MW01600984

murphy's

sonnets

james r murphy

first lines

033 once i settle down, i wait out the heat
034 once more the morning freshly sprung
035 one cold november when air was sweet
036 ornate argument flatters an open mind
037 outside my protectments the wild things live
038 rarely do i look full in your face to show
039 rather than singing your praises i write
040 research is like attempting second sight
041 riches are nothing without the heart
042 rocks have their stories to tell to the stars
043 try as craftsmen might to knit raw steel
044 twice told tales are rarely heard the same way
045 the time has come for more radical change
046 the tongue lags behind day's excessive heat.
047 the trek is finally well under way
048 the sundays of this fall seem far too warm
049 there's more to do, and now i feel pleasure
050 this then is my love's testament
051 the subway steps are cascading falls
052 the siren song of easement when i drink
053 the last of words should be the best of thought
054 the grey of dawn makes precious color's feeling
055 the cold angularity of cities
056 the bone-chilling sea rumbled in to shore
057 the bitter wet cold surrounds my blankets, wrapped
058 tangled lips will slur the will of love
059 there was a time when rainy nights became
060 themes are in the end ultimate chance
061 thursday evening brings the hint of change
062 tiresome reality intrudes most when
063 tired responses are rarely true to times, yet
064 tomorrows have scant to offer our hearts
065 time spent waiting becomes good time to be
066 this day arrives fresh to my lone senses

067 the will to be aware of complete needs
068 the walls reflect my gaze of open stare
069 the tight compression thus achieved is more
070 the slightest chance of sun brings out the best
071 the sense of fitness comes, it's here, there's no
072 the ordered process of form is bypassed
073 the colors and silver of old indian men
074 *they come to get you when you least expect*

076 the rush of change o'erwhelms my static soul
077 the room is stifling hot in my waiting
078 the rain seems incessant and sultry this
079 the old ways might be best for solidity
080 the leaves of the maple hang til the last
081 the furrowed surface of care is read
082 the echoes of last year ache in closeness
083 the atmosphere is oppressive this day
084 tis summer still and incandescent nights
085 hardness of image comes first from the stone
086 half hidden the form comes to idle mind
087 half the story of beauty is the hands
088 recognition of one's peculiar place
089 reckoning a loss with no thought of gain
090 another year, the bells still ring as loud
091 as i study biological charts
092 an augury of things to come, to be
093 the drums of death beat slowly in my mind
094 time's sporadic successes tire one out
095 tired from the constant effort to renew
096 a strange feeling suffuses this morning's rain
097 *purity of feeling flows from your eyes*

099 reeking of good times to come, revelers
100 half the sense of finding the core of craft
101 recent events seem monumental when
102 time has a way of permitting sweet thoughts
103 trails are for finding one's way in this
104 *the appearance of feeling is culture*

106 youth starts to fade as one thinks about it
107 there was a time she left behind the bar
108 the flesh effulgent works its way along
109 the truth of the matter is what matters
110 this late summer persists, as onward i putter
111 tears wind their way down these weather-worn cheeks
112 there's summer thunder promising relief
113 foreign feelings take their presence as fears
114 for most natural processes we take
115 for every natural green i've seen
116 friday nights i return, safe from the wars
117 full fifteen years since i left behind that
118 forms become elegant in their uses
119 formal adherence to patterned linkage
120 i felt the spring as i walked in the sun
121 i sit with a magic pen, capture thoughts
122 justifiable pride in one's physical bearing
123 just another day midst many more
124 knowledge gained is the being thought out
125 my time will come to someday and will stop
126 never mind how hard the concrete edges
127 over the pounding greasy city sounds
128 obeisance seems sadly neglected
129 green starts to come when winter melts
130 our dreams are all we have, butterfly wings
131 some things become buried in detritus

132 **nonacrostics**
133 i gather meaning when i choose
134 i pause to think, i sip my wine
135 i sometimes wake in the late morning
136 i used to chat up the women
137 i wear my hair long like the river's run
138 i would like to nestle on the bare ground
139 if winter is the family's time to talk
140 he seemed chinese, the glimpse i had of him
141 great gulps of wine remain, but then you're gone
142 early march warmth promises rain not snow
143 a gust of cold shrinks neck beneath the fold
144 again the wait, the halt, the old, the slowing
145 all that anyone has is his sidewise scrawl
146 all the ancients had their built-in myths
147 an arabesque within the whirling hands
148 and i a voice from greece then heard
149 carve out a place for your self
150 creamy turmoil slides slowly to settle
151 on this sudden fall day with its golden
152 my weathered face hides inside from the rain
153 my pride roars not, like the lion's kept tribe
154 my grandfather visited us one time
155 my eyes seek horizons these latter days
156 midafternoon drowsiness of place
157 spring's light rain is welcome, cool on my face
158 the background faded today as stories
159 the crack widens as i wander shore to shore
160 the radiance of the sun enveloped me today
161 the tongue i offer now will quiet speak
162 the sun has finally returned this spring
163 the timbre of his times marks the poet
164 the women peel themselves, and preen

165 there is a space for each of our own needs
166 the oil of midnight lamp dimly thinks
167 river calm, a slow slipping majesty
168 my coat finally adequate to winter's cold
169 there was a time when my blood ran hot
170 there was a tot of wine, now gone
171 and when the moment comes, it's there
172 this winter lurches on with a special timidity
173 time idles as i open my appliance
174 when hours move into the fall of one's soul
175 when i was very young i walked the path of autumn
176 when the evening meal approaches and mind
177 when younger i wished to talk to betters
178 winter will not wait its proper time
179 yellow stab of jonquil peeks through snow
180 all i have left is an occasional thought
181 seven imps improved their slippery grasp
182 a confusing fall warbler chanced outside
183 a poem ceases to be as soon as it is
184 long lazy western sunny afternoons
185 memory and sight are equalities
186 my passion has not time to spend, trying
187 small sapsuckers peer through dusty slant of sun
188 sometimes cambridge overdevelops her stalks
189 sometimes in january, sometimes later
190 the crowds have lain basted, spitted anew
191 the light is blinding outside my dank study
192 i come into my room, i come alone
193 i stand fast in this cold, this night
194 the sun peeks out from its place of growing
195 cock crows in my adopted father's yard
196 i was lying yesterday afternoon,
197 the order of brilliance is the web fresh caught

198 5 exploded sonnets

elaine choy's ode

199 each time we begin anew as a dream
200 each time we begin anew as a dream
201 loving before we have the consciousness
202 asking ourselves too soon about the hurt
203 in part acting out of those fantasies
204 needs reflected in their overt telling
205 echoes unwanted as we listen hard
206 chanting that which we most have told thus heard
207 heeding not the past we have both subsumed
208 our startled awareness brings back freshness
209 yesterday tastes tart as though new grown now
210 some semblance of order cannot be borne
211 our cultured astuteness standing tall proud
212 defending the depths we shall soon attain
213 eliding fulsome recompense we share

spring

214 to come fresh each spring is to be the child
215 to come fresh each spring is to be the child
216 open to the world to close inner form
217 patterning ourselves on growth's primal charm
218 asking how intricately nature has styled
219 madness returns as color brings morning sun
220 exciting the dormant feelings to life
221 luring vibrance with light's broad stabbing knife
222 arriving from low angle in shadowed run
223 corners of darkness gradually yield
224 health of unique, glowing, exampled views
225 appearances controlled as well as new grown

226 narrow byways thus slowly revealed
227 in exposing dark shunts to further bemuse
228 numinous reflection being the seeds we've sown

summer

229 the summer brilliance of noon light shimmers
230 the summer brilliance of noon light shimmers
231 our instincts move from that full directness
232 past the desire to absorb life's full heat
233 as we reach growth presumed in kernelled wit
234 madness itself is invited by all
235 enrichers of nature's bounty, we tame
236 love to bear better fruit as we know it
237 asking not what loose rankness might have brought
238 charge the sun with fetid air of decay
239 hail the dreaming green smells carried with us
240 along with sweating brown skin as we touch
241 normality flees reason in fullness
242 impending harvest has rhythmic season
243 night, never again be so far away

fall

244 the dropping off is unavoidable
245 the dropping off is unavoidable
246 our times run together, each separate
247 part keeps sounding as all the other's fate,
248 asking whether our fall is credible
249 mouldering ground as preferment seems sad
250 in formal last fitting of nondescript grey
251 life's peculiarity masking choosing
252 as eternal leaving what we have had
253 cold enforced in inevitable sleep

254 heart sore buried by bruised vegetation
255 again sense of never again never
256 night is felt not as abrupt cessation
257 in ordered schemas for forever
258 necessary essence is always covered deep

winter

259 the sky's malevolence presages shroud
260 the sky's malevolence presages shroud
261 of fast whiteness stretching to cover reach
262 past times no longer suffice as they teach
263 a leaden lowering has been allowed
264 massed consequence looms as ultimate
265 energy is focussed in dampening
266 life's force banked by winter happening
267 as sun's withdrawn symbol of final cut
268 cold, idiosyncratic, perverse
269 having formed individual barometer
270 afflicts all in soft separate ways
271 needing light again to hold off the worst
272 i accept center, flickering, final
273 nurtured by me alone through these hard days

i want to thank frank j. oteri for keeping me at the task of corralling all my sonnets and making sure i looked them all over before this book was finished. starting with the nurturing river poem on page 4 there are 14 acrostic sonnets which frank set to music and i have had the pleasure of listening to their performance on several occasions.

frank and charles passy (see pages 1 and 2) are old students of mine and now steadfast friends who share my love of poetry and they both have kept me focused on writing and publishing what i have written.

new york city in the pandemic year 2020

acrostics

full thirty and five years since the time
our days were joined, and the talks began
receptive to everything, you said, i can
full now of years i offer this new rhyme

reality begins the moment you're born
and ceases for self when that self will die
no easing that fact, i say with a sigh
knowledge of death leaves survivors forlorn

just remember the days when the newness occurred
our venturous paths criss-crossing their ways
the sheer joy of learning, becoming aware

each morning i rise with a questing bestirred
richness of detail, minable minutia of days
it's what i most treasure, friends with their care

murphy drinking raki at the turkish

time was when the fresh span of day sufficed
once dawn was sprung, growth was sure to come
carrying all the shining dreams along
hugging tight to secret heights of song

all i asked were willing ears to hold
reaching out to hear if what i said was true
listening with an awkward sense of dread
eager for the rush of secrets to unfold

sometimes though the air was stale with need
passing paltry effort at light mere candle flame
a feebleness overwhelmed by fearful dark

should i not remember how hard it always is
spading ground new tangled with striving roots
your many shoots green with the taste of spring

murphy sipping his guinness in his dotage, quite alone

the nurturing river runs in sweetness
of water's downward plunge, in a soughing
midnight wind of lulling call, in the lap
around the shallows behind around the bend

crossing when it's flooding tears apart the soul
inundating thrust in swirling thorough hold.
needing when it's trickling satisfies the mind
erasing disappointment in its filling find.

don't jump in the water pulling close apart
ease into the current flowing past the sight
seeking like as like in steadiness of will.

end the searching movement in constancy of thrill
tossing precious fluid sparkling in the night
arching in the aching spending of the heart.

the soothing slip to sleep in nestling arms
our expected end to reach for all new days
motion stills so the mind can skip away
and the ways we are meander dreaming's storms.

crisscrossing fears protect our inner screens.
inwardly moving, cutting shadows show
needs to be explored in learning how to know
each edge as vanished sight of soundless scene

doubts are projected onto a bursting shell
events unroll in waves of sense's seas
salvaged by their buoyance of crazed unreal

expansive holding unravels knotted hell
thoughts of love evolve in changing keys
as doors unlock in showing how i feel

towns grate around my bed their civil noise
offer vibrant stench in some peddler's fall,
mask a lover's thought in concrete of city hall
ask a calm acceptance in a doorman's poise.

crossing below my seeing is fitful stopping flow
in inundating web of forces known
next my very window this all is show
endless other windows searching for a key.

driving manic action, dust and roar and doom
endless other windows light with humming tune
seeking for the motion a sailor walks alone

endless are the changes the waves a deck will see
timeless in their balance of rhythmic changing moon
and endless folding difference cordoned off as rooms.

twice again the sun returns as fresh
orange wall beyond a slivery window's pain.
masks the crude brick in a pulsing fire of fleshó
a dancing ephemera of dawn refrain.

crossing in mind to room's controlling depth,
i note the somber pause in slow cloud's dance;
note again how briefly fullness of feeling health
entrances gaze on a sudden moment's chance.

down on the street below this quickened breath
erratic sounds remind of bitter scene,
shadows of the gritty gutter growing pale.

erratic thoughts all, grey images of death
tearing through this brutal clarity i've seen
alone above in soft ease of inward well.

the echoes of their voices are low heard
our dead return to the mind's inner sight
march in solemn tribute one more time
around the kitchen table after coffee

crossing on my plate's parading ground
in rough remembered line of lost years' flight
new patterns form in beat to now's salute
entrancing me with tiny trampling feet.

desire for all beguiles this unique strangeness
extracts in show the then of this pen's strength
sends searching sounds to test this moment's fate

each of us is heard a thousand moments
the thens of each our own repeating song
attaching bone to feeling rush of home

time again the clouds have burst, loosing fresh
occasion, the rumbling gift splattered harsh
morning with its slate grey thoughts, lives this night
as misty lights, probing halos of blind sight.

crossing wipers show my way toward home
inward doubts fade beside these hissing wheels
nodding love holds to arm; the thrusting storm
enmeshes swirling fears in moment's chills

deep shivers wrack my balanced act, my care
exhausts my seeming calm, the tears now come
senses reel as spray against the shell i guide

everything is touched within cocoon i bear
the outward shield so artfully spun is numb
as long as massive flood conceals, i cry

the pools lie stagnant in my mind, each one
only collecting water to evaporate
motion is denied except as disappearance
actionless thoughts fester without mention

crossing from puddle to puddle, i grate
inside, and lurk as lurching hulk, clearance
needed for my bulk; i, bumbling for a pattern
end in hip deep murky depths with no lantern

dragging for bodies pulls up bilious moss
every sweetness of liquid roils in this mess
surety of growth stops in this feeling.

each connection for flowing damns in its choice
the vital sharing of knowing is lost in my chest
all cedar smells are trapped, foiled in their sealing

the harbor is a hung silence of grey
only water calms to this balanced field
my directive purpose stalls, soul weightless
as the summer settles in, sun concealed

crossing sight's expanse, now fresh wholeness comes
in its sliding sense of time's demise
now again limits are just beyond limb's reach
each separate thinking stretching canvassed end.

drowning in color i'm lost in my mind
eating by seeing, i touch all of this time
seeking by telling, i make feel as i say

earning in closely packed sense of each line
this morning, though its message is only a day
an ordered sense of nothing, an otherness of rhyme

the oysters are too small and cling to rocks
our fetch is hard, and yet i labor on
my fulfilling is to earn this food so free
and so to share with those who live around

crossing through my mind's background, no clocks
indicating waves, concentrate of rippling on
now i need no more and end this playing sea
eking out my catch to hear a total sound

design insures survival as my ketch blows
east toward home, the tidal estuary
seething, moving cauldron strewn with dead homes

east toward sunrise, with water north and south
and tidal rhythm pulling, pushing, working
at my back, my fronts, i'm lost in the bay

this day's mildness belies it's november
our fevered storing haste is wrenched awry
morning slows til a summer's basking calm
asks mindless leisured joy in nature's eye

crossing fingers entwine our wishing's lives
inward doubts sluff in outward blissful clime
nearness presses all to the nearness smoothing palm
evening lengthens into warm seeing time

dropped from the shoulders our habits are open
each liquid moment flesh of soothing ties
stitched in quiet knowing to remember

each solid thought of closeness packed to cart away
tight to winter's quarters, when all will happen
again, and once again, in shared retelling sighs

tidings come in unexpected waves of fear
overfill narrow depths of emotional fjords
mark a surge of living flood in line of tears
attack, and crest in rumbles of creaking boards

crossings all ended in cul-de-sacs, angling
intersections become pointed break, moving
needed feelings come full, forcing, mangling
every future echoes in this damping proving.

details of message are lines of gritty facts
etched by water's passing; in ebbing's flow
scarred, fixed as final resting for this time.

each subtracting oneness is seen as regressive tax
the sin of knowing succeeds as a falling foe
and shows now in dis-ease, this telling rhyme

the sun i see corrupts my sight, i'm blind
only color of the mind builds up whole form
my fantasies are all i have, i bind
all inside, and hold to self with secret arms

crossing this threshold faults the visional field
inflying vortices pinpoint their shifting souls
nothing is cozy and feathered: nothing is real
eager nothing is attention to a particular role

doubts disappear in remembered ease of ends
edges blur til haloed stage comes all
silence draws its curtain to yield an inner sight

each other steadfastness can only pretend
to become freeness centered, certain to fall
accepting the vanishing me of my fright

the window is closed so wavy glass becomes
one link to all that's left so far behind
my mind constructs a wind to blow about
around apartment's sense of space in blind

crossing to inner self, a protective shield
in place, dropped before the eyes can see
needles of thought rebounding on the walls
etched as shown framework; end in furnishing me

despite green leaves, despite limb's dance
enmeshed in true earth's change, the sense of real
sits in this chair and orders all to be

enmeshed in time, cocooned in place, my sight
turned back to see the gathered host of all i've been
all astounds afresh with its patient waiting

the boat it is which moves the car we ride
our common chariot easing from its berth:
motion is seeing and felt in cold wind's search
as sparkling reminder laps at railing's side

crossing to the island, leaving man behind
inching toward being, quiet, protected, free
needing only self and finding it to be
endlessly enfolding depth in my love's mind

deep beneath this water pulses other thought
ebbing when it reasons, flooding when it feels
senses loosened like these glittering waves i see

etching in this day and its free wandering; caught
tied in memory of black and white, sealed
as totally moving love, as you, as me

this winter's snows are but inconvenient
on the streets, and seen, and of course, sloshed through
seeming at once wet, cold, and linked to you
evenings especially as i walk home

now there's some place to go, you see, and now
old dreams are remembered, and even some
recent hopes are revived, and to allow
idiot conjecture is no mere stunt

there's everything now, and your new-found love
accents my life, and work, and snowy shoes
my concerns at foot raise spirits above

effort is easy, achievement, a muse
so close that intimacy of shared thought
assumes concreteness as metaphor caught

murphy scooping butterflies with his net

though i shouldn't worry such as i do
over a triviality, the time that you're gone
since i know you'll be back., but when i'm alone
every childhood fear seems born anew

next time you're called unexpected away
on business we both know is busy
react to my plight, let me feel easy
in introspection, lose my usual dismay

there is in each of us a diffidence
at least as devastating as planned wrath
meandering through our daily actions

existence must needs have evidence
supporting and spotlighting each lone path
assumed by each of us as right, else rejection

murphy in the throes of early love

there will be times when i'm distant
omissions of affection will be the
scalpel, though cutting inadvertently
evidence of interest in other hunts

not that the quarry will be equivalent
or even equatable, it's just that
richness of tapestry embroiders flat
ideals-- love's not enough habiliment

the different stitches we all must sew
add texture, the prosaic deeds flesh out
more deeply felt emotions, make more of you

even your presence is not enough, no
some padding must be put behind devout
adoration-- vanishing point of view

murphy explaining his multifarious way of being

the old ways are sometimes not the best
ones, and new ground should be found for the plow
since i first practiced sowing, the spring's fresh
edge has blunted against time, become now

now when the tiredness begins to show
ripens to stifle senses, when the low
issues rise to blandness and we are loath
to replenish the basic yearning we've
always relied on to freshen our tastes
mouthing and rolling our tongues to achieve
each distinct aspect of creating wastes

since our senses seem jaded as of late
acquire new viands that might grace our plate

murphy consulting a chinese cookbook

tear from my breast that outdated feeling
overlook the fact that my heart is now yours
suppose for the nonce incredible sores
expose the rawness and hurt, revealing

needs we share and parts so exacerbated
our communality loses through pain
rightness of stance, depth of feeling, sane
idiocies we have make us related

take this scrap of paper home with you now
ask yourself why not myself along with
mordant images i've offered as love

enter my life as equal, assume how
special your hurt and my hurt make a myth
as we force ourselves to gather, to move

murphy practicing to be a troubador

the fire burns steadily even as it
overlooks its fuel, forgets sometimes the
source of all its strength, for it's there to see
especially in its warmth, flickering, lit

normality of occasion loosens
old fears, allows aspirations to
reach unhindered to a cheerful glow
imparting its visions, its muses

that's the truth of a parent's love
achieving the miracle of an other's life
mirroring selves made once more young

either you accept, allow a rise above
selfishness, or you don't, either one thrives
as cause and cause alone, or enriches none

murphy wondering as ever what women think

the spring comes slowly some soft sodden years
our long kept coldness trickles under sun
shining above somewhere (but here there's none)
ending our solid station, oozing tears

next will come the plopping green of a shoot
out of the sullen ground, left too long alone
risking its tenderness as the wind-blown
ides of march pass; it will begin, take root

that's what isn't seen as the cold rain falls
acquisitive tendrils explore
madness of subterranean tunnels

enhancing tendency in grasping sprawls
sending essence to meet that golden hour
as hoped for sun brings life to our runnels

murphy testing the river water with his toe

-of keenly felt desire, of that blinding
sensuality which resists unwinding
even in fulfilment, ah, i grow old

now my pursuit of love that sings
occasionally anticipates its end
raises the hackles and consternation
implodes, focuses a sense of things

the old fire rages and thick runs the blood
as maleness enforces its age old lust
my gender returns with a yearling's thrust
except now i've become a thinking stud

senses more balanced, now i feel more
actively engaged at my rutting core

murphy the heedless youngster

to tempt the muse requires a delicacy
of touch, along with a depth of feeling
shown, not by hurting so much as by annealing
edges, by cutting into blood to see

now i know that redness welling from me
overflows to stain the ones i touch in love
reaches even to those i pass by, to move
inward further, to draw gouts, a sea

to show the world that which pumps, how fully
are my veins to be plundered, how brightly
my images can gush forth in show, how truly

exciting the whole becomes when night
surrounds this often brittle blade
and by accepting this are my fears allayed

murphy preening before the mirror

two decisions i've made which have had the pain
of birth sit on my shoulders with dread weight
sadness etching the stony face of fate
ending the excruciating hoped for gain

nearness is such a palpable thing
overriding all sense of proportion
reason become shunned alternatives
in panic of engendered organic change

to end life for any breathing creature
admits the fear of the loss of one's own
most valued when least strongly held

eagerness in choice of one's future
skips that strength of how we might grow
aware of consequences, of trees felled

murphy leaving it up to the women to decide

tuesday night and the cold stillness shows how
our sudden thoughts look through from the blackness
movement ceases and the worlds of possibilities
are now with you the clarity of stars

rustling around my feet are old shades, torn
in growing past, as their fall and mine moved
alongside; in that dreaded coldness, forced
the pureness of vision could come no other

only promise me this as i prepare for
more effulgent growth which might not be curbed
ask yourself whether the naturalness
reflected in my leafy path this night
is wrong, whether the humus in making
assumes its role as inevitable

murphy settling into the new apartment

once when i was young i ran in the rain
down to the river, slipping, sliding down
each drop splashed into me, into the ground
free running slice in a free running grain

once when i was bouncing grin of the wind,
running fresh as spring's sweet morning mist
each leap was love, was life, was morning kissed
lightly kissed in rush round corner's bend

i see him now, that dart down long ago
space was morning stride, down to kiss the sea
arching in the shot to find the living core

once i felt like him, all at once to know
death is love denied, life is love set free
each and every morning the water seeks the shore

murphy after a hurricane in calm sunshine ripple

old air stains my lungs with its dusty taste
deep sighs meet sight of morning's wind-blown snow
early chores will be harder now i know
the simple things loom large yet must be faced

old dreams haunt, make my waking movements slow
each thought steams with breath, is whipped away
leaving soft unheard what i wish to say
i bend to tasks harsh as winds that blow

should this be the way i meet each winter day
a grudging plod in place of practiced flow
easy once begun and finished without haste

i don't remember when i settled on this way
needing no more than this, that habit makes me go
gently through the cold, my spirit steadfast, chaste

murphy warm in accomplishment floating free

old frayed shirts are my favorite to wear
deep grooves have become my memory's trail
each day i rise, loose moorings, set sail
trade flesh for fabrics i have chosen to share

old habits are not such difficult things
ever ready to hand, they are constantly there
linking already known to new instant, i share
i share what i am, my love has no strings

stray thoughts such as these, straight talk when it seems
appropriate enough, and what we both need
kept secrets i share when the moment will knock

i've practiced, you see, my glances are streams
notching the land and nurturing its seed
giving love as i live, weathering rock

murphy easing into retirement

once again pregnant sun dispels the mists
drops its light to enliven, to warm
enriches the earth with its returning charm
takes hold of dormant plants, insists

on bringing water from earth's depths, forcing
each leaf's unfolding tip of green; each fruit
living first in petal's bursting death
in pollination's buzz, in humming dance

since i was born this time refurbished me
added depth, cool pools of thought to drink
kind breezes to taste, fresh bold colors to see

in touching these my world became as mine
now i sense how things in passing pause to sow
growth in sprigs of nature this early day divine

murphy extending his metaphors as he pleases

once i settle down, i wait out the heat
drenched with sweat, listening for a sweet breeze
eager to think about how i might seize
the memory, so it and my being should meet

our presence is palpable to my fingers
etching the crumpled sheets with this my thought
linking pumping heart with what cannot be bought
it's the gift of flesh which lingers and lingers

should you ever ever again need my love
and you will for we all need the touch love brings
keep close in your mind how this day has gone

it's to me you should turn, and unflinching shove
next my door all that you carry, all those iffy things
get under my wings, you will not be alone

murphy reduced to everyday words for the sublime

once more the morning freshly sprung
despite the ache of parting
each bird i hear has newly sung
the song of spring its starting

once more the time is fully felt
each color burst in blending
light is red and sky will melt
i sense the heavens spending

she's where i go this working day
a presence pure and binding
kind wisdom said to inner ear

i skip along this concrete way
now-here is life unwinding
grounding flesh in words i hear

murphy singing his little heart out

one cold november when air was sweet
dry ecstasy with crystalline edge of sound
echoing hard crunch of fast frozen ground
the rustling woods nodded to a natural beat

one more time that feeling sweeps into me
exorbitant shock as remembrance of you
linking today with time past my purview
i feel that fresh youth in how i now see

since now has grown chill in pulse of the past
age beckons as clarity and grasps firm my hand
kicks hard both my shins and whitens my hair

i wonder how long this dream world can last
now that i know love's being this grand
growing hot in my heart space, misting the air

murphy dancing in full regalia

ornate argument flatters an open mind
deep analysis fulfills the willing soul
each time we show ourselves entire and whole
there are sparks spent bright newly to find

once early, listening, your feelings i heard
each glance of your eyes stirred, prickled my skin
love tasted my heart and then tasted again
i wondering, reeled, all my senses absurd

such mixing of self is admixture of selves
and this starts in at time pairing occurs
kissing and touching as the cat when she purrs

i trust all this now and add books on our shelves
needing and tasting with sweet twisting tongue
giving and taking each day while it's young

murphy synaesthetic as the next man

outside my protectments the wild things live
dining on small things as big things will do
eagles eat rabbits and the wolves caribou
the polar bear eats all the ocean will give

outside my mind is the wind and the cold
etching my thoughts with their presence sore felt
leading my dreams to your warmth which will melt
inturning fears so our futures will hold

since my home is now safe in that it feels
as you laughingly greet me, more and more warm
kind to each weakness and molding my strength

i look out my windows and past all the seals
note how their presence distances harm
gifts reaching arms appropriate length

murphy jumping through his usual hoops

rarely do i look full in your face to show
a throat hunger huffing wildness within
curt in speech my eyes then let you know
how much i care, after that i ink my pen

each morning yet the sun comes brighter still
love creeps, then leaps to eye in liquid glance
you cannot more truly show your will
openly for the other as a mating dance

unless we freely share each other's gaze
as home we sit alone in candle's glow
reaching snuggled fit in heat of water's pull

each evening now i face fact of fading days
my choice is be and never utter no
each night is flashing lights, breezes full

murphy at the piano bar of love

rather than singing your praises i write
a more telling, if cooler, approach from me
closer to actual feelings set free
heedful and careful, i bring you my plight

each time you find your inner glee
like the way we get at night
you dimple eyes, look straight at me
absorbed, aglow, aimed, and tight

good lady fair, fire, and fire again
each time i'll laugh aloud and sing
reaching back to you each time you touch

on cue from you, to sing your special song
down deep in voice to tune the room
exactly to our shared heart's noise

murphy with a messy room to sweep

research is like attempting second sight
a question visits past its birth of time
cancels drift of mind and begins to rhyme
herds bubbling thoughts iridescent to light

each time i come to know is such a bursting swirl
linking moments my glittering eyes will see
your taste of blood salt, tongue tingling to be
almost chocolate in sweetening of the world

growing to this point as we both have done
earns laughs and joy for the rest of it
rich scenes ahead are our map of love

of what more we earn in our long time sit
declaring life turn full after its noon of sun
easily shared, and fitting as hand in glove

murphy batting first again on his mythical team

riches are nothing without the heart
as deep within my throat i find my song
could there have ever been a better art
here now at finger tip and hardly wrong

early now in the morning's freshened light
looking out windowed booth of this our ship
your bringing joy with your welcome sight
a warm greeting issued from your unmade lip

gone in the past need for an enhanced sheen
ended the time of artifice on show
rather the touch of hand, unexpected, warm

our time together, thick as it has been
defined as cello bowed a heartbeat, slow
etching its melody as this day's charm

murphy afloat on the baltic sea

rocks have their stories to tell to the stars
as they wait cold through long nights of the earth
cold clots of matter, liquid at birth
hard now, unchanged except slowly through scars

each time i find another one, i find passage
looking hard i espy some scabrous rock
yielding through presence its glacial massage
an inexorable change, a gouging, a shock

great stories have an essence whole when told
echoing hard in ritual memory's runs
remembered exact in quick tongue's hold

old stories still most often the best ones
drawn out slowly, retold, til strongest are worn
exactly in happenstance, around neck, reborn

murphy being his own psychiatrist shaman

try as craftsmen might to knit raw steel
or wed copper pipes to half-filled reservoirs
artists imbue bronze with the sense of real
draftsmen give paper thin right-angle scars

elegant gallery walls stand bare
left to lesser lights, ever ask yourself why
escape from the safety of your executive lair
shrinks to naught from thirty-fourth floor sky?

assail yourself while watching agile men screw
new I-beams into ever higher place
daring to fall from their majestic view?
ever tempt your gravity of inner space?

risk the anger of your artistic peers
stop stockpiling barren years

murphy meeting a muse in the flesh

twice told tales are rarely heard the same way
old sensibilities are slowly changed
as my fingers twiddle in nervous fray
doesn't it seem odd not to be deranged

even now as i sit back in my chair
looking over my recent histories
each succeeding step on personal stairs
seems inevitable inward foray

as i sit tonight and think tomorrow
needing yesterday to show me the way
down to where i should be made more aware

elasticity of time is sorrow
rending my position so that today
seems already lived, all ready to share

murphy putting it all in order

the time has come for more radical change
old forms were best, re-thought, and then passed on
as i practiced, sharpened as with a hone
directed toward what when new seemed strange
even grotesque, absurd, impossible of smooth rendering
laying down aa presentation a rough
escutcheon which couldn't be polished enough

so now it's done-- a fulfilled labor of love
all things must end and so finally be
nothing more than phases, recurrent themes
derived from the peculiar human mind
ever inventive and yet forced to see
relics, and forced to build upon those beams
sent from past lights-- we're all partially blind

murphy fashioning a shield to hide behind

the tongue lags behind day's excessive heat.
oddly reticent to keep pace with my
ardor trickling from forehead, it drips dry
drinking this sultriness, chewing salt meat

each scratching scrawl grates, sensibility
lacks purposeful life, my quite adequate
ends shimmer into shades, meaning is cut
skewly from whole cloth, sewn as probity

a lounge is all i ask, cool wine and time
news brought by reflecting what's been before
discovered slowly as protected place

evening charging its easement with muted grace
resonant trueness of tone touching more
surely than mere exercised reason: rhyme

murphy popping the top of a cold one

the trek is finally well under way
our early planning but brown memory
a look toward the morning sky today
deepens the sense i will no other be

either i was too afraid before we met
letting a natural sloth prevail, or
else it's to you alone i owe my debt
starting from wishes to have come this far

a gift of life can never be repaid
nor can breathing, once started, stall
double knotted our futures in a twin cascade
elevating dreams extensive, held in thrall

roads behind the travelers forward gaze
stay tracked the same as when the dust was raised

murphy in the race for the longest of hauls

the sundays of this fall seem far too warm
obsessive in their clutch of summer green
at once so untimely that they demean
destined change and thus unnaturally harm

even if we wished and so could achieve
life as endless joy and bounteous growth
even if eternal perfection were both
some thing and all things, the leaves have to leave

action always implies different ways
new climates, new ethics, and always new ends
doubtless also it requires a new me

each one i've left behind, each year, all days
require that part of myself which transcends
self to assume life now as memory

there's more to do, and now i feel pleasure
over the problems and the reasons for
attacking them, to add existing lore
doubtless answering my mentor's measure

existence is described, and thus pinned down
lifting arms of delicacy when deftly
expressed, my wings of fancy solely
standards of individual renown

as i progress in my feelings toward
necessary form, a peculiar pattern
deepens the obviousness of what i do

each man does this in his own time, a forward
rush of unknown force, no time to discern
simple motif of constant wish to renew

murphy the bulldog who refuses to let go his bite

this then is my love's testament
ordered and sent to you first, then others
and it's not the gathering that bothers
depths of quietude earned by wordy bent

else why bother even to set down pen
linking leaves of a yellowed certitude
else why belabor obvious attitude
striking rebounding anvil times again

at least i'm in my mind as i think back
needing the impetus your presence gives
daring to expose that i dare not say

endlessly striving to fill my mind's black
readings, those modulations it takes to live
sounding those inner depths, the protected bay

murphy telling his son to play by going up the creek a mile or
so

the subway steps are cascading falls
our collective fears smell fetid and damp
a spring-like spate becomes slobbering sky
deep inside i keep heart warm and dry

each time i look i see life's walls
lost memories limned by mind's fresh lamp
etched deeper yet by this time's flow
such depths attained, yet how far to go

are you listening still to my occasional word
need i speak again of my bond to you
drawn tight today in my havened thought

each time is now in your presence sought
reality becomes the mind's purview
sends tremors and tears-- seen, felt, and heard

murphy sopping in a drafty auditorium

the siren song of easement when i drink
our call to owning up to laziness
as i age into a dim senescent gloom
don't you always bring me back to think

every time i bring the brimming cup to lip
letting loose the slippery sense to be
each empty glass brings new songs to me
such pourings as one should always hope to see

and let's stay on this course we've set upon
now that old age and wisdom shares the way
don't leave me now that i've discerned that play
exists in all we do, all that you still add to me

reach deep for springs in fresh new day
sent to color dreaming bliss of morn

murphy a guinness in his prime

the last of words should be the best of thought
or one's ink is dark and sore lacking life
a dull totting up with a neat round hand
don't you miss all my metaphors caught

else when was where the books were found
lying open with their speckled seed
elsewhere was when focused force was first
singing loud with a drum of sound

a little finesse when it circled round
new forms chewed, now well earned taste
digging within the old to break new ground

each attack a rout of a self, sewn, bound
round the pattern so deftly obscured
skirting the absurd, in a ballroom, gowned

murphy climbing a well known hill

the grey of dawn makes precious color's feeling
old wounds fresh ache in sitting, seeing how
a touching time unfolds its artful healing
deep thoughts that glimmer full are with me now

each time i wrote before i wrote beginning
last thoughts of what i lost in heart's hot squeeze
each time i write is now in all its meaning
sad framework with its bold romantic tease

a touching time implodes a total message
new notes are strung on strings in fingered guise
dark thoughts are seen as moorings with no ties

each time i scribble scrabble brand new passage
returning to the start i note the skies
see somber shadow spread the day's soft eyes

murphy up at first light and ready to go

the cold angularity of cities
old wrappers crumpled to be tossed aside
aspirations becoming gutter pride
drunk again with my sending you ditties

else when the joy was all on the first
living of the dream which now overwhelms
else where my notes were firm personal realms
sent with sense of place ingrained in the verse

afterwards i stripped my feelings in form
noted the passing of love twice again
dreamed a bit and let fantasy become

ever more refuge from ecstatic storm
read again the lines of mine to regain
self and uniquity in modern day rome

murphy beating a dead horse once again

the bone-chilling sea rumbled in to shore
offensively driven there by the wet east wind
as i trudge this cold edge my mind makes a blend
doubts of the future and clear cries for more

every meeting place should be such a mixture
letting variant moods clash round one's heels
ejecting broken shells of below surface meals
seining raw life for meaningful pictures

at least that's how it seems in retrospect
nobler, clearer, a remembered sight
doubly etched by recognized need

even now while troubled with new prospects
returning scenes arrive with such force, fight
seems hardly in order to a soul so freed

murphy driven sane by the rhythm of the surf

the bitter wet cold surrounds my blankets, wrapped
old thoughts intrude into the warmth i find
a pattern once developed stays within the mind
deepens until it holds a lifetime, mapped

each debt we unknowing start by starting
love again, and yet still yet again we do
etches skin with a tattoo colored new
seizes absurd hold on sense of final parting

as i late this day remember where the strife
needled through the bulwarks thrown up in my young
desperate haste, i wonder if i've been true

each year since then, beginning with sense of you
reveals itself in each these tries, each upward lunge
shows how early, late, i sense in you my life

murphy swimmimg in amongst the icebergs

tangled lips will slur the will of love
once tripped the sturdy rock will change
all know who know to know the strange
deep within the yielding cove

extra touch for free this rush of thought
like bombs up high, above the night
each bursting glint a tamping tight
stretching the soul so it be caught

addled brains amiss, adrift the scene
nestled within what has always been
demanding attention as to what we've got

endless flarings fresh with new being
rash and sure like a teenage dream
sexy, and charged, with an intimate plot

murphy cool, breezy and sunny at the beaches

there was a time when rainy nights became
old friends, seeped into my collar and drew
attention to similarities through
deepening puddles at bottoms of soles

each unseen tear of humanity's poor fools
listed in wind, slanted feelings as i
eked out that pleasantness we all try
sensitively to manage without shame

answers were to be found in my inner
doubts which were dry and protected from wet
events, from that encroaching soaking dark

old habits were formed, the confirmed sinner
rinsed his head, but kept the safety of pet re-
sponses, buttoned his coat to hide spark.

murphy in the eye of the hurricane

themes are in the end ultimate chance
of message, understood by bone and blood
pressing home the feel of what else is good
after it's all over with magic dance
mild friends together to mention how few
easy answers were pursued, how many
lives were touched in love; how often when he
asked to be, how seldom did we give his due

cold burning was his firm request of us
handing, as it were, residue of love
as aspect of his deeper self alone
needing tradition not, nor hallowed dust
in choosing how 'twas done at last, to prove
naught but to be forever dreamed in stone

thursday evening brings the hint of change
of surcease from the drumfire of pressures--
partly for the cultural weekend rest
and partly the choice to step aside
marking a certain time as pertinent
eventually, and repeating that
link to expected gain of insight, life
and even love accentuates why

choices are always made in patterns
hearing soft echoes of remembered thought
acting out of previous unfelt linkage
neither the unknown beginning of what
inside we haven't learned yet clear to see
nor the past we've left should stop our changing

tiresome reality intrudes most when
our defenses are down, resilience gone
painful impingements increasing bright tongs
assailing our protectments, our sins
memory is our process as we deal
evening the background and all the hurts
loosing good reasons become efforts
assuaging wrongful guilts for how we feel

calm recollection then permits our lives
health, allows growth as inevitable change
asks nothing more than acceptance of now
nothing less, nothing else can ever give
immunity from those fears whose felt range
nurtures our instinctive probing to know

tired responses are rarely true to times, yet
obvious in their flashing of secrets
permitted roles never offer surcease, but
assumed as resolvement; they're never whims

meant to highlight by indirection, bounced
edgeward in outline, getting words edgewise
little is gained from postures learned as guise
as children: habit precludes new-mind sets

cutting through to trueness involves despair
haunting in its memorable response
asking guilt instead of that fresh wonder

needed to produce change for which we care
instead of surety we should seize chance
narrowed option as concept is blunder

murphy not feeling it yet

tomorrows have scant to offer our hearts
our present intrudes with its sense of time
protrudes as an immediacy, as a prime
accusation, the now the sum of parts
mixing the pattern of our agos and our whens
each moment allowed to slip away
lives as waste discarded, lives gone astray
a jumbled heap grown from our might-have-beens

calling for change will not force it to be
hard breathing only underscores the futile
attempt at shaping what should be formless
no one can embed a sudden memory
implanted indelibly as subtle
normalization of our humanness

time spent waiting becomes good time to be
ourselves, alone with indeterminate
possibilities, becalmed in ornate
appreciation of the moment we
might ask of time in which we find the time
each moment means, whether inattention
lets in feeling or even if mention
allows the sense to grow to reach one's rhymes

children innately apprehend that mist
hanging before the next important thing
assuming vague outline as our harness
nearness becomes important, not the gist
intuited of life, but the wellspring
nestled securely in our awareness

this day arrives fresh to my lone senses
opens feelings to blue expanse and sun
pushes past experience to bring the one
aspect of life which erects no defenses
magic is change without cause or reason
except as an explosive inevitability
luck is confirmed as system so vast as to be
a happening: we approach proper season

clouds are punctuation, sprigs are thrust
health is leafy warmth of our next full growth
as a certainty the memory allows
nascent identity is begun in flesh first
in full openness of touch, in being both
needed and giving, in growing strings of now

the will to be aware of complete needs
of ordered words which echo primal
possibilities will in the final
analysis sustain itself in written deeds
mornings are my best times as my mind clears
each wisp of underlying fog of night
leopards that prowl beyond determined sight
and yield glimpses only of spotted fears

clean slates aren't clarified as butter is
heated just below browning level, kept
at room heat thereafter without spoilage
nor is erasure forgetting except
in details of carefully plotted foliage
needing only light to grow again in bliss

the walls reflect my gaze of open stare
obliquely, leading a fluttery lid
past the topmost hindrance of latest bid
at loosening the self and being aware
mirrors couldn't do the same, for their light
engages my thought at total image
leaving nothing to imagine or gauge
askew, to further confuse orbs of sight

confusion, thence it comes, that full felt
health of focus with what has always been
at hand, but denied by definition
no lone individuality can ever be dealt
ideas enough to re-present the scene
needed to engender re-creation

the tight compression thus achieved is more
often for me dwelt on as the punch press
permits a proper definition, stress
accumulated past usual time's store
meaning impressed past tolerance, as form
eventually understood by the mind
lived again, again to help me to find
a cohesive meaning within the storm

complexity has this siren's appeal
herding what occurs toward the squalid
acceptance of control from the liquid
nether world wherein we natural feel
in total submersion are those solid
needs we have so often successful hid

the slightest chance of sun brings out the best
of me, that i might be heard, or perused
perchance enjoyed as this rather bemused
athlete tends to hide his inner wordy crest
minding how seldom the light dawns when shown
evoking a charitable faith in that
luster of bringer only, not what
after all separates our flesh from bone

cold achieved goal in desired act of faith
hot felt welling shaped to fill inner mold
aching hurt buried hard neath muscled strength
needing the sight of those whose assured grace
is supportive, heard alike, even told
now how muchly needed and to what length

the sense of fitness comes, it's here, there's no
other world to be joined to than you, whose
proud insistence on your self attested due
allows at last my careful plotted show

my deliberately profound deliverance
easing into a carefully loving relevance
life become joy, not to be set aside
as mere being, so that time be misapplied

chalk a fitting circle, plan your headlong spell
have a weaving chantment bring the heart
as well, make your every moment count

none will hold you closer than this human shell
in those deepest places of his soul apart
neath his self protectment, lies the whole amount

murphy plaiting a friendship wrist band

the ordered process of form is bypassed
our chaos imploding in dense inward
progress toward that center in the words
ascribed as a forced telling, the harassed
memorable complexity of that
eventual payment called as our right,
leavening our flat ardor, the so slight
actionable cause accused-- in effect

cursed as whimsical chosen chartered show
held in check so as to heighten tell tale
aspersion when released-- i do not see
needless pretense as manner to bestow
issues with human hurt-- we all shall fail
naked awaiting warm propinquity

the colors and silver of old indian men
one night they decide their sleep won't come
pull their serapes tight round to find some
assurance their ways matter still, have been
mattering since the early patterns were fixed
exposed as costume and thus the role they
looked to to explain, they dress to meet day
as and when it comes, their plumage does the rest

cold steeps old vapors as body expires.
heart seizes, then knowing stops as the balance
assumed stays, and the kept warmth slides away
nature sometimes shows itself in layers
icy rime holding all life until brilliance
notices the numbered few who are still today

they come to get you when you least expect
overt movement against the impressed needs
pardonable but expressive of seeds
aggressively rooting for their effect
mention of the short attention we span
erecting the ways to reach that after
life which so controls a lack of laughter
assaults a proper balance, the command
calls into being an order, the felt
heavy burdens carried as fallen foes
attacked successfully before the remorse
needles the senses, stitches the wounds dealt
in caring past the normal reaching lows
nameable and thus palpable in force

the ordered process of form is bypassed,
our chaos imploding in dense inward
progress toward that center in the words
ascribed as a forced telling, the harassed
memorable complexity of that
eventual payment called as our right,
leavening our flat ardor, the so slight
actionable cause accused-- in effect
cursed as whimsical chosen chartered show
held in check and so heighten tell tale
aspersion when released, i do not see
needless pretense as manner to bestow
issues with human hurt, we all shall fail
naked awaiting warm propinquity
the form is what i miss, the effortless
order which so constricts the turning in
patterns balance and the aweful new sin

added as awareness is easy to confess
martyrs are made by hand as a unique
endurance of gained response, agreement
lurking in our strongest purpose, the meek
acceptance of our deepest fears, our rent
clothing as uncontrolled cover, habit
hard put to veil what we so most would have
as love, the openness so stripped in partial
noticed rhyme that reason is slow to grab it
insanely, and thus to prove pain's needed salve
nothing more can so begin to startle

the rush of change o'erwhelms my static soul
old stones stand shattered, old stops are gone
proud props of comfort stand if at all alone
aloof almost from efforts to keep me whole
my flywheel slips loose, the choice, if made, to
end any of the careers that might be
leaves me the poorer somehow, which i see
as damned if i stop and death if i flow

cordons or cartons, the fences remain
horses are ridden and control assumed
action implies directions and the ends
needed for movement; and those are the chains
in my heart, the dreams of completion doomed
nitrogen welling, blood, decompression bends

the room is stifling hot in my waiting
old fantasies slip soft under droopy lids
part of my life slides by as changing rids
act of control, emotion creating
matter as here and palpable in mind
each aspect of the nodding sense of scene
lives floating, as the wispy motes careen
attach themselves to eyes as they go blind

change becoming fixed and fulsome happenstance
hops past control, the will to become real
at last, the loose shreds of doubt defeated
neatly enjoined in affording a chance
in the thousand or so at hand, to feel
newly tasted as savory soup, slow heated

the rain seems incessant and sultry this
odd june, drumming on carapaced moving
pelting the unwary adventurer, 'tis
a strange and wonderful plan for loving

mark that occasional storm front as omen
electing wetness as witness to twinned
lives commingling, mixing with their god sent
allotment of form a blurring sense of wind

couldn't the very fact of this recurrent
heaven sent congery of messengers
answer each spray of whispered doubt

need we protect ourselves from those torrents
if indeed they lead to enriching dangers
needing our mutual strength to plumb their depths

murphy always carrying his umbrella

the old ways might be best for solidity
of dreams, giving flesh and form to thought
purpose in measuring wit til it be caught
added to, girdled tight as fixed ferality

minding the wickedness in probable sin
ending fantasy as it is allowed to flit away
leaving gloss as a memory which then will play
as polished scene, a recalled and historical been

countries are shaped by the will of few men
hunted over as privilege, retained as feudal right
anything but a sharing within their felt boundaries

no notion of why, no question of when
is more appropriate, what seems to be quite
normal, whether life is love maundering

murphy accepting his birthright of serfdom

the leaves of the maple hang til the last
of the others, their time has been, the raking
promises nothing more than ordered heaps
awaiting fire or trundling truck to come

maybe this clearing signifies that some
event is in the making, that in our deeps
looms a singular feeling which breaking
away from solid roots blows; will be past

chance argues for the number of those leaves
holding unique possibilities being
anything but unlimited, in fact

nothing is usually noted as a lack
in the lives of those who are partly seeing
now what some have already felt time weaves

the furrowed surface of care is read
only as the seams are made, deepened
plains scored with the sliding wet of tears
adding rough troughs, and when flooded, silt

masks are worn by all men in dead
earnest, as basic aggressive weapon
louring, a ritual grimace of fears
anger personified, preserving power

i trust my life, trust the face i offer
hard at times, almost sullen my silence
bounding in its practiced stoic strength

nerveless in surface texture, and all for
invalid reasons misleading, the sense
none has yet to see is felt at last

murphy carving a false face out of a living tree

the echoes of last year ache in closeness
of image, the sun and table seem sane
poised in the mind to underline gain
accepted slowly in my verboseness
made somehow to be much more than what is
etched so trenchantly in expectation
life itself assumes such subtle direction
as to make mockery of other bliss

crayons can scrawl as well on borrowed sheets
have indelible patterned thought subsume
a blank future, and wielder of these thoughts
needles the senses to produce small feats
intended to furnish a spacious room
next to the heart that's saved, tight and taut

the atmosphere is oppressive this day
our collective wills stagnate, hang fire
pose as solidity of purpose
a scattering of sins forecasts our guilt
morality is our common aegis
enriched with peccadilloed curlicues
lifted together in polished phalanx
accepted as final proof of each worth

couldn't a chariness break through those clouds
hanging to stifle with sense of closeness
a delimiting of common canopy
needn't we force a personal freedom
in case we can break through the accepted norm
noting thought as peculiar totemed soul

tis summer still and incandescent nights
of town beckon to footloose shambling stroll
perhaps tomorrow will never come so whole
as thoughts alone sift through haloed lights

maybe blurry skies are the only goal
even lonely stars cannot serve for all
lest commonness itself become the shawl
affecting gentle march to lasting cold

coarse laughter rings from out the open doors
headlights mark paths of habitual flight
and signs stand mute to point the various ways

need there be obeisance and thus no more
is asphalt so irreversible, a terminal path
nothing can move me toward you tonight

murphy walking the night away in new york city

hardness of image comes first from the stone
as we shape its mass by diminution
releasing the fused strength of eon's sleep
ordering our eyes to compelling form
lustre of surface comes from within as
deep rubbed horniness of hand, the patient
chipping of calloused roughness, the chamois
half felt, half sweat of creator's old dreams
ask michelangelo how he loved the
life lying under, which he always showed
endlessly furbishing his time, his world
freeze your fluidities as he has done
fix form for all around you to be seen
thrust your sense of space into that source

or you can work in more pliable wood
sanding to finish a perishable
having the grain of life enhance, make its
appearance as counterpoint to soft
possibilities of rot and decay
ephemeral beauty has its place then
trying our acceptance of the loss of
heart which eventually takes us all
either course is right, of course, and both are
windows to beauty, allowing aspects
of our yearnings to hold the attention
rightly given the most human of wants
let your eyes see for us those yet hidden
dramas in all blocks of unshapen worlds

murphy chipping away at marble

85

half hidden the form comes to idle mind
as musing revery muscles my will
running my wishes to that which i feel
obliging a respect of humankind
lithe shapes return, torment my waking dreams
deadwood twists the scene walking on the beach
charwomen reflect their polishing reach
harmony is achieved in solid terms
a small sculpture can be much more than stone
lying in my hand, and turned round to see
effects of light and weight, as work of art
firmness of image can never be shown
for what it is, the remembrance to be
takes time to burrow down next to the heart

otherwise why wait to say what i felt
standing in the room reacting? my words
happen now to describe the sense of absurd
as i came close to flame to someday melt
perhaps that's what it is, a future heat
encysted on special optical nerves
that retain those unforgettable curves
held somewhere behind eyes, and thus complete
else how explain their strength of return?
why else would they seem so much purer now
old traces, old glance, old remembered grace?
reach back to that, sculptor, and make it burn
light my hoped-for past, and somehow allow
dark thoughts of my world to take proper shape

murphy sanding to refinish his oak floor

half the story of beauty is the hands
attempting what the mind sees, feels needs
reconstructing in solidified deeds
of time, caught in its own shifting of sands
less is formed than we imagined was there
doubtless for the obstinate nature of stuff
coming to hand as we sit in our rough
hoping for telling what we would lay bare
as we attempt to show what we should think
lurks within ourselves, we always find in
exacting what we wished to draw forth, whole
form, the completion as a smoothing link
forging what we wanted with what has been
the medium we work with, and our soul
our falling short shows most the strengths of the
surrounding solidness of what is there

how can we presume to achieve a rare
alignment of what is caught, and what is free?
perhaps we shouldn't even try that which
eventually can never be done
the effort seems not to be worth the friction
hardly glimpsed between mind's rhythm and pitch
either we take what we have and feel right
when we allude to what we feel might be
or build monuments to our frustrations
remember, as you start creation's flight
lightness and clarity are figments we
demand for our incomplete reactions

murphy reluctantly giving advice to an elder

recognition of one's peculiar place
in the whole jumbled human scheme of things
changes the contours of cherished ego's face
halts the puffedness self-vanity brings

as this site becomes more fixed in the mind
revamping direction of forward thrust
doubts present themselves as some sort of kind
benevolent friends, and as such, discussed

until that certitude of position
loosened the quivering gut of doubt
lying beneath my social condition
i, for one, was timid in my thought

expect ease and contentment only when
the individual adjusts to his own den

murphy practicing his scales, training his hands

reckoning a loss with no thought of gain
is foolish neglect of a learning tool
churlish eschewal of that mindful rule
hidden causes if found can save the sane

as i take stock on this second go-round
recording my hopes for some future time
doubts of rosy beginnings are my prime
bills of lading, holding feet to the ground

unless i miss my guesses completely
life will now be less than what i first felt
loading my expectations with young trust

it shall perforce be smaller, more neatly
executed, though cards no better dealt
the hand shall be played with more telling thrust

murphy pontificating even back then

xmas 1970

another year, the bells still ring as loud
crispness crowds all sense of sloth from my walk
health beams in the cheek of all curbside talk
rightness is redolent, the world feels proud

it's that time of year, and as usual
simple goodness never seems quite enough
the purposeful purchases, balls of fluff
meaningless toys; and giving is dutiful

alacrity accurately contrasts with laziness
softness with strident recurrent themes
positing tinseled glitter as spirit

outlandish as it seems, feeling outlasts
embodiment of feeling, my thought seems
more real right now than all augmentation

murphy digging deep to find the mother lode

as i study biological charts
meant to explain an intricate plant's
existence to any half-hearted glance
simplicity is lost in all the parts

symbols, cut-aways crowd the sense.
a horrible specificity stands
grossly for what when seen in summer wood
exalts the moment, makes one drop pretense

fortunately i can pick and choose
renditions of my corporeal touch
opening myself when and how i want

maybe that's enough if i wish to choose
my hard-won clarity of stance, and as such
exemplify a successful front.

murphy untying his knotty self

an augury of things to come, to be
ushered in with a proper panoply
gives a fitness to this small gathering
uses this occasion to further take stock

simplicity of purpose and style
takes precedence when untangling complex
thoughts, our statements pointed and felt
here, in this place, at this table, right now

enjoy the warmth that we sometimes bring
take from the others some of yourself in return
hear us talk fumblingly of what we feel

importance is defined by time's choice
remembered in outline, retold in dreams
doubling intensity of this, our life

murphy writing an occasional poem

8-3-74

92

the drums of death beat slowly in my mind
one measured step comes hard upon another
lesser men seem content with all this bother
yet you and i tremble before that wind
not enough say our fibers as they pulse
not enough to react with each our tears
etch your skin with corrosive scalding cares
cascading from flown canisters accursed

hammer the nails grown long in pampered ease
attack the spittle of our leader's lisp
let yourself see the red promised in your eyes
efface the proffered posters mouthing peace
fold not your flaps to dive and flesh encrisp
fly fresh against that wind and die, and die

time's sporadic successes tire one out
options sap what little reserve is saved
looking closely at consequential braved
years adds gnarls and whorls to limbs now grown stout

neat denouements have always been denied
night people; their maunderings are never
ended; rumpled sheets are seldom clever

clean wins are morning paper sports applied
heedlessly to coffeed haggles tonight

and i remember-- when anew i greeted cold
light of freshness, when certainty i felt
echoed those long nights before, when the tight
force became overwhelming, when the bold
force of youth tasted its triumphant guilt

tired from the constant effort to renew
old fires as ashes grow deep in the pot
little men go out and leave some cold, few
youthful bits of charcoal as what they got

nothing should be left as we fight for those
needs we perceive, else the very holding back
ends natural rhythm and will foreclose
coveted chance joys won in sneak attack

how else deceive the flow of body's sag
as gravity grabs and eventually wins
life, and pulls our very hearts to the ground

even as we blithely try to play tag
for the joke is on the ones who count sins
forgetting that flesh is bought pound by pound

a strange feeling suffuses this morning's rain
crying world reflects harsh rippling surface
harmful torrents wake in light's dim grey pain
rousing one reluctant with lack of purpose
it's not the same without you by my side
thowing in your wonder reason for my being
taking in the glory of this ritual's guide
moments strung to adorn the neck of fresh seeing
a greyness is grown expected now, background
shadowing a blurred existence of shame
paring sharp edge to welling, oozing thought
once before you salved throbbing, lonely wound
ego's fence, battered, broken in your smile's claim
marking everyone with your child's lesson taught

family no longer a feeling in time
occasions outlining odd moment as ours
remembrance as only touching-- this rhyme
earning its presence in its trueness to yours
love in its absence is feelings unshown
interred in this morning's imaginary mists
sunk in the present, i'm drowning alone
alone with your image conjured in wisps
murky at waking life gradually stands
unknowing in its realness, so felt as is bone
rapt in its nowness: my mind sees your form
please don't forget me as once we held hands
hold to our oneness as we live alone
your life is my present to me in my home

purity of feeling flows from your eyes
one small hand resches tentatively for mine
each garbled word you say is mulled wine
that enraptures my questing, it's the wise
rightful place you seek that allows my space
youthful growth, i should always take my place
first in profound awareness of your love
one's acceptance of freely given life
registers when least expected, when heard
exactly shown in childish scrawl shoves
light into those dark fears which cut as knife
inside myself deep, down where stars appear
saying you are the one and only goal
as i stumble forward hoping to keep us whole

maybe you don't perceive the storms which blow
ever stronger in the world we will live in
surely your thoughts are yet before your pen
and not half behind as mine are now
maybe you will grow to say what i can't
using what i can give as proper route,
reahing ever upward and inward to doubt
pleasantries and force truth in elegant
high form, i trust you will, i also trust
your presence now and do not choose to hide
only open myself to what you are.
neither of us understands what we must
heed if we are to succeed as allied
entities in a family not at war
read this over when you will have read
those other limners of the inner soul
hear my anguish as i reach for proper role

in your life (and mine) for we both have bled
reach if you can the rough truths we so fear
disturbing lest they rise in their hard way
become so heavy they begin to play
into fantasies of escape from here
right here is where i belong and will be
that is if you can still find within your heart
heart's room for mine, i now know that reason
draws us away from what is plain to see
a life, a love are precious hour by hour
your growth and change now become my seasons

murphy bewildered, stumbling, blinded by his fears

reeking of good times to come, revelers
initiate proceedings with their noisy touch
turning to good purpose their sense to blush
under all their skins in kinship's cellar

a coming together in that bond of blood
life squeezed to lividness in a natural lust
leapt upon with a driven, sweating musk
yet timed and restrained, a small social pond

perhaps paella is metaphor enough
as we sit, installed in all our differences
each of our appetites to be assuaged

lift up our wine then, chew with a fine gruff
lightness these fresh prepared portents
a needed melding of steamy life engaged

murphy hosting bookish friends on a sunday afternoon

hector maysonet's graduation poem

half the sense of finding the core of craft
even when the skill is inner and not seen
comes from accepting the worth of practice
the essential rightness of self control

otherwise strength is dissipated
running through fingers to soak in the sands
muddying only the spot apparent
and beneath one's immediate place

your personal worth gives the other half
sureness and form, when hands become cups
of solidity holding that water
needed to reflect individual form

even then, of course, those peculiar bumps
that go with each of us complete the scene

murphy readiung his acrostic of the year's valedictorian

ronald bradshaw's graduation poem

recent events seem monumental when
old memories are compared, so we sit
nailed to this moment thinking much of it
and heeding not what it took to get here
life is filled with these glorified features
despite their essential normality

but sometimes the immediacy deserves
respect, and high points reached enlarge our view

achievement real and earned is such a time
drawing this group together in homage
spotlighting a young man's glad mastery

his gracious presence here today brings such
a pleasure to each of us, i can only
wish he would honor us again sometime.

murphy holding his own at the honoring banquet

jackie turner's graduation poem

time has a way of permitting sweet thoughts
their fulfillment, to grow past experience
just as desire for spring flowers, cold months
ahead of their coming, is more than hope

children are our own special time machines
keeping personal erosion of faith in check
allowing the yearned for colors existence
transmuting any past sense of failure

the torch of striving passed on
unfelt until we come to understand
remembering is more important than now

now when they don't yet perceive the freshness
enmeshed in their efforts, and unknowing
receive the glory of unprovable dreams.

tony chisholm's graduation poem

trails are for finding one's way in this
odd terrain called life that we've been placed in
trying to make sense so as not to miss
out on previous traveler's tracings

nothing prepares us to read those bent twigs, signs
yielding the knowledge of passing only
clearly there should be some broader designs
highlighting our path when we take lonely
issue with the elements and their force

since you and i are for whatever reason
hiking in the same vicinity, remorse
over this obscurity is shared, open lesion
look on it as a visible soreness
marking the refining inner furnace

murphy fighting with one hand tied behind

to senorita mesa who looks at me with obsidian eyes

the appearance of feeling is culture
one acts to show inner content
schematizing chaos, giving hints
else the receiver never feels quite sure
nailed to this ingrained need is deception
order for the sake of an assumed role
rigidity of response taking its toll
in plainness of love, in pale conception
that's why the way you looked at me tonight
and last night, and the night before them all
messes with my mind in marvelous ways
elevating my responses past tight
scenarios played with complete recall
all the way to a forced creative haze
which envelops my senses and cuts off
help in the form of expected reaction
old habits are sluffed while new renditions
lift from the underskin, become that stuff
old cocooned crawlers spread in sun to dry
offering finery of wings from where
kinky hairs once undulated in bare
sordid gorging with never thought of sky

104

as i sit with you and are shown these things
the depth of those obsidian eyes which
mark my soul pulls me down to that instinct
excepting all serenity-- that brings
with it the preservation of the rich
individual sense of how to think
that gift is a full overwhelming love
holding forth receptivity of my
oddness, do you know whereof and why
black despair should disappear when i shove
sadness over the edge of those two pits?
i don't, and will admit so first, and shout
dumb sounds, and chance to tell the world about
it, the feeling strange but it sure fits
and that's my song, inarticulate, brave
noise to draw attention to freedom
earned not by strength of stance nor learned response
yet embodying strength and learning, save
everyone you see, my love; take from
some, but give to me your all giving front

murphy lengthing his stride yet keeping his formality

youth starts to fade as one thinks about it
escaping from each of us while still prized
as a natural resource, utilized
rashly in a seemingly endless chit

the realization of its end takes
honest appraisal and an acceptance
rarely evinced, yet full of poignance
evoked while in one's prime, and the heart aches

elderly feelings have their place for the young
they force the growth needed for mature thoughts
heading, as it were, forward to that place
respected by all: a wise seeing sung
expertly by one who balances taut
epitomes of youthful strength and aged grace

there was a time she left behind the bar
our revelry was joined instead of stoked
she'd become the victim of a coughing spell
as winter weather found the frailty in us all

laughter was the language that she sought
living large the wit of bar room talk
yet again we meet, but with her now as friend
pleased at last to have her in our fold

each time we meet will now be more than fun
reaching for the moment best that we might know
sipping slow the loosing liquid of our thoughts

it never fails to bring surprise within its wake
close friends who gather thus will come again
our need is time of sharing with those who care

murphy working hard to keep himself afloat

the flesh effulgent works its way along
our afternoon of boozing now upon us
sounding thoughts that now can feel so strong
and waving hands that make quite loud a fuss

let us all now know the why we're here
lady sal lets us each to know we're rare
you never saw such a careful pour of beer
pulling gently on the knob to share

each one of us to cast our glance upon her
ribbing each ourselves in quite her special way
seeing from on her side the worth of local folk

i do not think myself so much a special bloke
cause what can i, a codger, bring to play
of course, if she should wish, i would demur

murphy crazy as the loon he was

the truth of the matter is what matters
our perceptions circle that frail outpost
most as the mind breaks continuums just
at the wrong rhythmic juncture, so natters

recoil into meaning, and then delimit
growth as a logical extension, allow
a spansion to be assumed, buildings now
relegated to solid though filigreed cement

ending become so pertinent to onset
that patterns no longer need ongoing
allegiance, choice has become creative thought

nature has no boundaries, so we set
newness as hedge, inevitably sowing
eternity with awkward sense of plot

murphy, ten years old, wondering if he will ever grow up

this late summer persists, as onward i putter
old trash of thought rustling around my feet
each time i turn, again a new day to greet
light fitful rain is washing the gutter

is this the birthing ground, the fundament
sent here to swirl, then coalesce
and i sniff the wind and willingly say yes
to rainy days and puddled wet cement

old thought recedes more day by day; and now
electric absolute, not held at bay
lives in new forms, new final rooms

i think again, and thinking, feel just how
sense will return, a bit more day by day
a bit more summer proudly, lately, blooms

murphy finding nature wherever he is

tears wind their way down these weather-worn cheeks
offered unbidden as i walk the dog
deep into the central park sense of fog
elements out of place between brick peaks

beaten down earth now has no growth, no green
objective before it, to send gendered essence
rising above the crumbly loam, to dense
aspiration for approval in being

how times have changed, i much prefer back when
morning presaged that life would be fulfilled
out of bright cerulean cloudless sky

remember those days when might have been
sundered reality, reconciled
eventual death, almost made one cry

murphy flexing his broken wing

there's summer thunder promising relief
outside my air-conditioned secret lair
hunched over my writing table with bare
existence as my ultimate belief

little escapes my fanciful memories
ending always as marvelous future dreams
neat denouements appear in the steams
hissing from the now wet street histories

preparation for that change from summer
renderings, from baby fat to lean look
interrupts at most inopportune time

now the world seems quenched, the past a mummer
crying, a costumed newly sharpened hook
equally keen in point if stated or as mime

murphy reading smoke signals he sees in the skies

foreign feelings take their presence as fears
in our actions, forcing maladaptation of
self, making the syndrome of isomered glove
hang in our face daring frustrated tears

once before i came to that position
understanding nothing but the awkward
task of somehow turning inside toward
out by nervous and besotted volition

friday mornings i woke early to bring the
weekend closer and modern doubled rest
altering brittle edge brought by felt strangeness

then monday permited the safe re-entry
enfolding that alien blot as welcomed guest
receiving the new restoring to old sameness

murphy trudging along his alloted way

for most natural processes we take
our initial understanding from past
renditions, handed down as truth at least
layered with cant and forebearer's mistakes

a case in point is grape made to wine
until you asked me how and why the change
reasons for ferment were to me too strange
in themselves to account for a taste so fine

eagerly i pursued the task, to learn
more about this everyday event
asking more and more the complex questions

readily enough i came to discern
kinks in what seemed logically unbent
suds and foam instead of neat equations

murphy chem lab specialist extraordinaire

for every natural green i've seen
some from chemist's hot bubbling tubes
though red from heat, become verdant in indoor light
simulating that sap transformed by sun

as city life adumbrates my sense of smell
a new awareness comes when i sniff the wind
the art i see on sterile sunless wall
outlives the primal colors it once was

judgement of existence imbues my sight
contagious auras shape my chosen way
existence tinged with a tempered guise

now a wattage forces the night to let me see
the control i've won, predictability
brings a range of choice complete with whys

murphy an indian in an urban environment

friday nights i return, safe from the wars
of privilege, not mine so much as those
reckoned to be without, who thus impose
their problems as sore salt on all our scars

heavy that tread toward haven of home
ascending front stairs leaving feelings behind
the door closes softly and then peace of mind
forgets the cost of that closure, and from whom

one's fireplace crackles an unneeded warm
regal dog lolls near, close by petting hand
the smells, the sounds, the tastes are all one's own

hence my surprise at the niggling doubts that harm
and bring the final fillip of the loan
that's callable if panic hits the land

murphy listening to news about ebola

written a couple of months into my tenure at lower east side prep. i was
living on kennedy boulevard in union city, new jersey. cuca and i lived in
a mansion built in the teens of the 20th century by a german lawyer
complete with punching bag and barbells in a small basement gym. we
had a black standard poodle named waco. i was waking up to the fact i
couldn't save the world.

full fifteen years since i left behind that
other sensibility, that full fledged
righteousness of position, that hard edged
civility of the aristocrat

little did i suspect the end of my
youth would correspond with the beginning
do-si-do of a more subtle sinning
eyewash used to cleanse the stigma of sty

good men and true hide behind their
attitudes of ethnicity, or their tightrope
balance of neutered feeling

light could, i suppose, allow these to see
if they were disposed to do so, tossed to where
no underlining of position would be revealing

murphy in his first year of teaching math

forms become elegant in their uses
our presentments following felt secrets
rising to do bidding as we allow
meeting needs silent in slow radiance

showing basic outlines, shaping that softness
lying at surface of fluent shifting
ensures sharing sole sense of what we've been
telling stories as shadings become ourselves

today has lost freshness but gained surety
in small editions of realized loves
nothing can replace that already lost

gaining comes in giving sense to might be
going by letting past be understood
opening by admitting perplexing now

murphy the old existentialist

formal adherence to patterned linkage
oaths unsaid with tacit penalties
restrictions accepted to foster growth
our fatal togetherness palpable

under shared tent, simultaneous sky
reaching down to touch mind's razed in being
chosen feelings filtered through common lens
each moment a newness of shared life

rarely do we choose to accept nature's
etching passage as indelible past
masking our feeble attempts at control

often we neglect how meaningful words
need attention to echo in future
years as intensely felt essence, our truth

i felt the spring as i walked in the sun
felt the ground stir beneath the concrete walks
extending to curb, to street, to park stalks
likened to nature by this city's son

that isn't the way that i used to be
this thinking change beyond my feeling sight
harking to symbol of change, this delight
encompassing the mortality of me

should i then decide to leave wretched place
putting my toes once more into warm earth
raising my eyes to see unbroken fields

it does make sense knowing length of this race
neatly short enough to show this life's worth
grows longer through immediacy of feeling

murphy adjusting to an urban environment

i sit with a magic pen, capture thoughts
sensed as completeness, loose them in telling
i sit with a magic hand, weaving doubts
tossing chances into air, catch them, flailing

i sit with a magic tongue trilling songs
words formed in felt order of their hearing
that sing of rhythmic secret stirrings
held focused as my message for the young

a magic for me is lacking in free
magic when its endings sense is coming
a magic for me survives in growing

ghosts don't haunt my mind's gnarled old tree
but i sit midst magic objects, midst mumbling
crowded images born now in their showing

murphy searching for the perfect rhyme

justifiable pride in one's physical bearing
as meaning, is quite often taken as another
notion, misunderstood; and does often bother
even the confidante of what we're wearing

more times than not the way in which i feel
fails in translation, the height of my lips
undermines my utterings, whose hot tips
resound with unintended force and appeal

though attention to detail would seem apropos
honing one's appreciation of the effort behind
summery facade of ginghamed good health

oh that it would, oh that the depths below
depths assumed the righteous form we've outlined
ever more singularly as our truth and our wealth

murphy offering advice to a young woman who asked

just another day 1970

just another day midst many more
united as all are by expected sun
noteworthy perhaps as the only one
elected by chance to pass into lore

elusive thought that, commemoration
ignoring great men, and no kind words for
god or his supposed cohorts to scar
holidays with men's perorations

that's for everyone else, or at least
enough of them to make me doubt my own
eminence, or is it perhaps yours now

nestled behind these thoughts brought from the east
today lies an importance, but it's gone
home where it belongs ere twilight glows

murphy celebrating the ordinary

knowledge gained is the being thought out
in proper attentive frame, captured then
through process, sketchy trail signs having been
marked in singular mnemonic ease of route

it is explored carefully, this new field
life assuming fertility in careless chains
linking unexpected ways as the grains
evolve from edge to center to yield

reason guiding the prudent hand, reaching
sense in urgent glutted feeling forms
past old manners of blindly seeing

on a changing crystal, a crusted teaching
each existence is fresh finished charm
miming eternal moment of being

murphy expressing most of it in words, but not all

my time will come to someday and will stop
yet now impinges on resolution

turns attention to slackened existence
ignores pattern for mystic scenic drop
meandering past benign assumptions
established as a too ready presence

when life becomes a decisive proving
it's almost always a non-knowing spark
lighting irreversible path to dark
laughter at the sheer impulse of moving

cheers become an automatic response
outdistancing performance as the true
moment's measure, inverting sense of new
ending inexplicability of the nonce

murphy smoking cuban cigars and blowing smoke rings

never mind how hard the concrete edges
extend the corners of habitual beds
walk among the alleys as your hedges
youthful dreams become gutter shreds

or is it only filth pumped from smoke stacks
raining on our souls as ashen arrows
keening in their cumulative attacks
coating our feelings to blackened marrows

is it too much to ask for human-kind
that they learn to live with nature's changes
yearning especially for the unexpected purblind
obviousness of thrusting mountain ranges

doubts as to our entire programmed being
exhibit themselves if our eyes are seeing

murphy wearing out his shoes on the sidewalks of new york

over the pounding greasy city sounds
beyond congealing midwinter's cold
extending my thoughts which know no bounds
my inviolate heart would your soul enfold

your remembered grace transcends the scene
visible beneath my three-story abode
as i sit to formulate words i mean
love's like that you know, when distantly bestowed

evoking fine tracings and big fat loops
needing but my time and finger's movement
this essential message jumps through hoops
in the way of all contained improvement

new times shall come and new words be said
ere the external world and our love be wed

murphy choosing chocolate over roses

obeisance seems sadly neglected
down 'mongst the more common of us folk
either there's no need for folderol, or
there's brightness of serge to carefully hide

only sometimes i want to break out, and
allelujah until my lungs quite ache
letting whomsoever has such a mind
acquire the recognition of good men

need i add that i see you too few times
necessitating truncated forms of
address, elliptical patternings of

gruff speech; forgoing that special reverence
each human life should receive when approached
limited as ever our lives but our own to choose

nurphy winnowing his stacks of manuscript

glebe's shoulder

green starts to come when winter melts
leaking its white covering in spring floods
ending the howling bitter wind when pelts
bushy with warmth moved through the woods

each noticed gain toward fulfilment
summer's promise, growth and maturity
seems cause for an inward humble kneeling
hope for this small bit of earth's surety

over this farm's more or less acreage
under this beshingled old roof
lives the promise of the mountain's courage
declaring growth's harshness as enduring truth

expect nothing less than this artless plan
richer in spirit than ingenious man.

murphy born in the cold of early march

our dreams are all we have, butterfly wings
nascently spreading to dry, unable
to lift a heavy weight of solid things
how could they support success that's stable

each evanescent fancy of man i seek
seems to soar away on sails of trust
in every quest i catch, i turn up weak
xerxes whipping the sea for being unjust

the rarest gem is mined, one grubs, until at task
each lyrical fantasy becomes an entirety, a whole

every young poet should have such a mask
neatly foreshadowing his goal

the hunching caterpillar knoweth not
how logically inopportune the plot

murphy understanding the foolish nature of counting coups

some things become buried in detritus
of living too deep for germination
moiling in subterranean closets
elastic fading in a vain snapping

they suffer neglect of purpose, beings
held from rooting, hard shelled kernels
in murky hovels, forged gemlike hardnesses
never permitted consideration
growth and change forever denied
such an adamantine protectedness

but sometimes when outward skeleton creaks
etching one's age and loss of another start
careful sifting of that infertile loam
offers small reflections of what we were
memorable in their compacted facets
easing life's logic of one-way passage

murphy stirring up the compost

131

nonacrostics

i gather meaning when i choose
when i follow one path, not the other
i constantly choose, i greet the future
accept what trundles to its meeting

i am the sum of memories stored
i have always feared the choice
the necessity of chance in being
bringing time's forced change

i have always examined my life
as i carefully lumbered along
found the future of all my choosings
reflected upon them as mirror pool

i often feared doing the wrong thing
but found mostly that i helped others

murphy sweet-talking the gatekeeper, after hours

i pause to think, i sip my wine
i look to see, the river, the sky
all there, world-large, it's mine
all i see is all the reason why

my friends are gone, we all get old
rivers snake downhill, wind tickles trees
this is life, this, my only hold
this afternoon, this summer breeze

enough i say, for such as i
scribbling here my prescient eye
i seek only to be this here

enough to know, to stake my claim
to mine this moment with thorough aim
life itself the atmosphere

murphy on the balcony looking out

i sometimes wake in the late morning
drugged, with sleep hardly rinsible from my eyes
the sun's brightness, preternatural
i struggle to right my perceptions

heretofore i've been able to accomplish that
transition from my dreams to my self
as slowly i assume clean habiliment
as limbs respond sluggishly to will

i suppose it is the inevitability of my face
the control, an eschewal of loss
integrity of position... that's the morning

which causes conscious choice to be
light of growth, light of possibilities
as new won shell reflects its subtleties

murphy rinsing his face after shaving

i used to chat up the women
get 'em off to a bar booth, quiet
sip some suds, begin the blather
we had fun back in those days

i learned to speak to the young
get 'em to see certain things
sip some thoughts, think them through
we taught each other how to learn

the gift received, the paying of attention
the lifelong embodiment of focused self
feeding the mind's insatiable curiosity

the gift given, the full rogue uncle mode
offering a boost up and good advice
keeping notes, records of what we then did

murphy beginning to keep a journal

i wear my hair long like the river's run
down gravity's trail to reach the ebb and surge of sea
my thoughts grown long, long past my own brief time
down imagination's bends to mind's reflective pool

i keep few clothes and those are worn too thin
i eat fresh food i forage for, but limit such
i drink too much, the dulling liquid stills
an old man's pains to ease him through his day

the books i read blur slightly now on every page
the songs i sing scratch throat and hoarseness comes
my broken hand goes numb when used too much

my time grows short as i dodder on the paths ahead
i know not what will end my days nor how soon i stop
and here i sit tending to this morning's task

murphy not giving up the fight just yet

i would like to nestle on the bare ground
as the sparrows do, as if taking a bath
together in simple companionship
the sun, the occasion, the interplay

i would trust the mindless gregariousness
the underlining of shared pursuits
even if the apparent gain was nothing
more than time of simple feeling joy

never mind the mites beneath fluffed feathers
the gnawing individuality, the itch
which must, perforce, be assuaged

that singular concern of bodily well-being
is rarely perceived by outside
watcher of instinctual flock

murphy stir frying the evening meal

if winter is the family's time to talk
rechewing what summer held in its teeth
i'm preparing now for the coming winter's sleep
in day's collapse of glory, in evening walk

if winter, when it comes, will stretch to fill
the time of complex story exactly told
so all can hear and wonder how to hold
the earth itself; to quiet down, to listen, still

i would hear the stories of those who know
who've lived life full and long enough
to tell it straight so feelings show

i will wonder fresh a coming white of snow
of cold outside the human snugly cell
the growth a child would know

murphy grisly with beard

he seemed chinese, the glimpse i had of him
he took away your slow stepping thoughts this night
your reluctance at parting was of a piece with mine
spring was in your dress, i watched you out of sight

we had talked the whole time through in fits and spurts
with tail chasing circles back to where we'd come
back to where we were always headed, you and i
the adding up til the answer, the final sum

a breeze unites this world, it touches everywhere
no matter how softly, we know it moves
completely around to touch our other sides

it brings the smells of all the different lives
it lets us know they are all the same inside
we carry whole our parts, and parting's how we share

murphy easing into a sense of his own worth

great gulps of wine remain, but then you're gone
the crumpled door of your chariot creaks shut
the winter night closes over our worlds
one we share apart, one we share alone

i'll gulp this wine tonight, the part that's left
this restless prowling thought i can't escape
i'll chew the scenes a bit, and hit high notes
i'll weave my blanket soft with telling weft

i'll think upon our fit when we are one
when all else slips away and we can be
as loose and free in mind as feelings charge

i'll sit and stare outside to tips of tree
so bare and thin this freezing time of year
i'll wonder how our love has grown so large

murphy feverish in his hot cloudy room

early march warmth promises rain not snow
an aged chariot has whisked you away
i turn, face the heavens before i go
back into recesses, back to where i stay

the formless yet becomes, my hands will
find it out, type the blood that's pouring
from life so felt and true, the life lived still
still learning with the young, still soaring

i turn, feel want grow large within my chest
my breath brings an inward expansiveness
a breath ever filling, let loose soft as sigh

i turn, touch earth again, moccasined and proud
pony tailed and aging, putting nothing by
walking ever lonely within my mind, its crowd

murphy newly knowing why he lives

a gust of cold shrinks neck beneath the fold
reluctant steps lead down the slippery bank
in need to find the moving water's soul
kept purpose focused, steady, mind on hold

dawn is just a moment still to wait
all is hush, time waits full for time's new birth
the red of gold starts up from eastward flowing
i wade right in and make my flesh its mate

i wonder fresh an old eternal question
why downhill run will lead to highest thought
why do we always send our roots to earth

when what we want and wish as station
climbs above, invigorates the all that's sought
insures that eyes will elevate their search

murphy awash in river's glory

again the wait, the halt, the old, the slowing
the look aside, the slouch of pain, the knowing
game played, blood taken, hope clung to
a while longer, time is short enough as we go through

i guess ahead, how long is long, how strong is health
but mind focuses now, this room, this smell, this space
the awful thoughts, their persistent prowl of stealth
the lastness of the sterile hospital, the sorrow of the place

outside is cold, march continues a slow wintry pace
the snow still there, begrimed with the urban air
we all live here, the people of poverty, the children of wealth

emotional wear brings its awkwardness, the loss of grace
we are all ground down by time, malfunction, we all need care
seeking with fearful frenzy the maintenance of ill health

murphy, his only medicine left, the touch of hands

the tongues of men

all that anyone has is his sidewise scrawl
his lurching stab at style and full form feeling
to grab the eye and make a heart's healing
the rhythm of the writing is the drawl

for all that's said is made so it is right
the comely sound to tip each end at ending
so it will be just nearly so to spending
the graceful slur of punning pen, to write

to write so well we shudder at the sight
to see the deftness go from left to right

and then there is the quiet tongue
the long-forgotten mother's tongue
at mother's breast, the early tongue
the tongue of mother's breast at night

murphy never losing his texas accent

all the ancients had their built-in myths
exemplifications of what they could not say
forthright, as you and i are wont to show
our understandings of inner feelings.

they could hint in safe established modes
what they could feel, no one asked if choice
were guided by some deep. darker intent
than what ostensibly was a retelling

i suppose every evocation of life
is shared with those who went along before
this massed accumulation occurred

i suppose these words are a type of song
remembered by some forebearer as his very own
peculiar interpolation of mine

murphy understanding that logarithms are power

an arabesque within the whirling hands
the ones that grasp to sing their joy
i want there my soul, and inward held
i want a panoply of sorts of things

i want a herd of awkward giraffes tall
i want a squad of penguins waddle small
i want a swooping troop of hawks from height
i want a leaping snarl of bees in flight

i want a simple untold thing to be
a net of words to still hand's plight
of how to sing lost memory

i want a simple issue i can see
in twist of tying hands to sight
in pledge to all that is: to be

murphy having climbed to symmetry

and i a voice from greece then heard
that roused me from my stuporous state
a blinking light, a whir, a click
a voice so quick, some time, i'll wait...

another week and i'll still be here
in slothful, bearded, somnolent bed
alone and tossing those last nights through
will-less and care-less with thoughts of air

tomorrow it starts, again, it starts again
and i will soldier that last week too
on and on slogging to keep my place

that fate will change for now i know
what you feel, and said, oh so briefly though
i miss your soul in same room's light

murphy thankful for the telephone for once

carve out a place for your self
where you can simply relax and be
but not a place of ease and rest
quiet, yes, but all in all a busyness

time for a wandering mind to roam
and space to pace in the thinking of
this is not the place of serene quietude
so much as a creative solitude

to search the self for its wanton vibes
its truly, really, want to know, its grits
but not a place of frenzied haste
so much as the splendor of certitude

to weigh understood possibilities
to heft the data field, decide

murphy leaving clean swept his trail behind

creamy turmoil slides slowly to settle
i fiddle around waiting for the taste
but first a pad to sop what foams over
the full pint presented, dark and delicious

the polished stone cool in its veined glory
soft chatter of sots a murmuring din
the third and fourth are smoothness embodied
charlene the maid stands steady at hand

why do i come here to this haven of brogue
to prattle my nonsense and think of the world
why is this basement the paragon of pubs
luring the thirsty with its kindness of pints

charlene the maid graceful with another
and i understand place as the warmth in her grin

murphy ginning up the words as is his practice

it's september today

on this sudden fall day with its golden
death but a suspicion of things to come
each breath tastes crisp of sudden whole time
full harvest of dream is now coming true

once i felt as strong, quick, as sure as sky blue
restored to its throne through air stripped of grime
each sight tasted ripe, each sight tasted plum
life giving its all withholding from none

now i know to love as well as i can
before it all leaves and cold rules the world
tasting ripe fruit of fixed nature's plan

just when we know how good it can be
just when it all meshes as wisdom's teeth
life slow shuts her gates, waits for the spring

murphy canning cling peaches for winter's dessert

my weathered face hides inside from the rain
pelting slate-grey early fall weekend day
it seeks surcease to decrepit decay
an easing of the crinkles underlining pain

my self thus sheltered from the ceaseless change
dancing in the puddles glimpsed beneath my room
perched upon the window seat, i am home

my house is shared now with electrifying young
voices trilling in their trying of the mind
it vibrates health and happiness in kind
exuberant sticking, testing out of tongue

my place remains here now, the new is always strange
bouncy in the interest of the unfolding bloom
tossing in the breezes conjured in this poem

murphy mixing the markovian chain of inference

my pride roars not, like the lion's kept tribe
bringing tribute to a lazy master
demanding through slow insolence portion
befitting unnecessary provider

it stands prouder still, as a quiet drive
lean hunter gathering gifts the faster
to forget the getting for, the notion
of praise subsumed in joyous non-ending

life, that is a vision of simple sort
for such as i, self-effacing trueness
of purpose, resonance as melody

the song not of forced singularity
but of irrepressible rhythmic pattern
to engage all but the most tainted taste

my grandfather visited us one time
when i was young and we getting settled

in the new house our cat gave birth in bed
with us three oldest boys, in an honored place

the low mewling woke me alone in the dark
wonderment at such a plaintive soft noise

i slowly reached to see what foot of bed
might yield to make such resonant chord

the slippery round smallness of form felt
it's opposite, there was no hold it seemed
to slide away from touch yet cling for all

its thrust became alive within my hands
and quietly i led through darkness to find light
and safety in my seeing small breathing life

murphy remembering how to conquer fear

my eyes seek horizons these latter days
they lift concerns from near impediments
they free perspective to encompass life
that trackless way of imposing form

descending brightness becomes an inward force
pinning the past, focusing on traveled paths
to the seeming completeness of faded orange
the tinged totality of lone extinction

i reflect on youth as ebbing ensues
retrace my movements at source
they betray assumed pattern as destined birth
and guaranteed newness in each day to follow

i will note such varied shadowed understandings
as those future suns repeat their ordinations

murphy writing poetry in the principals' meeting

midafternoon drowsiness of place
sun slants through thin-curtained plain window
flies hum and crawl cross splotchy shiny floors
the sky outside and wood below are joined
here, i shut my eyes and wondering gaze

through the warmth and stillness
past my feeling for fences arbitrarily between
feral reality and security

the amniotic fluid must have been the same
the effortless, buoyous, dreaming comfort of surrounding
warm skin
that's the precise distance the world has come, as have i
through the stretching and soreness
through overt hostility, to this calm room

murphy settling down for his hibernation

spring's light rain is welcome, cool on my face
a red light stops my slow ease of thought
looking i see stream steady with cars
a river of movement come flooding and full

i remember a time sitting in place
watching a fish line by keeping it taut
the sound of the river, the light of the stars
eternity caught within a darkness not dull

as nighttime surrounds my now as my then
the moment expands and bursts into dreams
to love that i feel, and how all things might be

the light turns to green and let's me now see
how movement of rain is not all that it seems
how fullness of feeling is all that has been

murphy stiff and proud in his tiredness

the background faded today as stories
will when told, an occasional sharpness
limning reverie completely out of hand
distorting the completeness of that now

i content myself with sipping green tea
and its hint of oleaginous aftertaste
concentrating on the heat of moment
in the hidey hole of the sole of me

tomorrow i'm promised newness, return
of hopeful presence, a taught burgeoning
tamarind to taste as delicacy

ritually i pay this time its due
declining to elaborate future
and disposing to batten up what's passed

murphy the old vicarious voyager

the crack widens as i wander shore to shore
becomes a chasm just outside the door
what i lugging take from chair to other chair
is never quite the all that i will ever dare

there's something left behind no matter how
i make my petty lists of what to do
there's something else i need in need of now
something left behind that keeps me from the new

i've tried to heal the wounds tearing me apart
salved my inner fears with liquid numbing lethe
sleeked my outer skin to hide afflicted heart

though i know i've lost the peace of elder's sunlit heath
i know i've kept the angst of youthful stab at art
so i order still my steak and tear it with my teeth

murphy exercising the only muscle he has left, his brain

the radiance of the sun enveloped me today
as i walked the long brooklyn blocks alone
the sweat stung my eyes as i strode on my way
the fullness of life seeped deep to my bone

i gave over my thoughts to the sure smell of you
as i heard you tell how you grab hold on to me
i gave over the world to close in on this view
i felt your strong arms squeeze health into me

i saw your beach dress which never will drape
i heard your sweet laugh sweep up in your throat
i sensed your new thoughts not yet in your dreams

my feet left the ground, my hands sought your shape
i reached for your hands, i swam for your boat
i thought to myself, how strange it all seems

murphy with his lopsided grin

the tongue i offer now will quiet speak
the song, the rhythmic sky are words of love
my tongue slow teases taste in ample proof
your lips grow full in softness ruby round

the song i sing transfigures our first parting
the taste, the then is sparrow on my breath
my words seal now as blood passed to another
disappears to flow alone remembered red

the sounds i hear remind of senses flowing
the lips of love retell the sad sweet dream
i love you alone of all the others

the softness now surrounds the dark of night
the lips of love in parting grow anew
the lips consume the all envelop me

murphy waking to cuddly fetal form

the sun has finally returned this spring
hidden behind the rainy clouds too long
the warmth too strong for withered flesh
to bare itself, sit outside, sing its song

so here i sit in this cushioned bar room stall
hiding in the cool from fiercely sodden heat
i nod to the barmaid, a frosty one, tall
i sit and sip, snug, my retreat complete

no bugs in here, no mosquitoes, no wiggly things
i'm safe and sound, and can stand another round
another think, another try to understand it all

why the fear, why the curl-up inside, what brings
me here, to this dead end, this mouldering ground
this final street, a cul-de-sac to unclimbable wall

murphy sane and reasonable in his certitude

the timbre of his times marks the poet
delimits the deafness in his ear
or hers, or theirs, the lonely readers
who faddish flock, comprehending, hear

particularity in the voice of the singer
signifies a shirting of his soul
or hers, or theirs, the lowly hummers
who fearful wrap with burlap whole

the style we each assume creeps early
slithers hard as habit's hips wrapped round
tucked and gathered in life's movement

the arch of leg and arm's sky stretch
show what was found the first time through
in an acid etching timeliness of view

murphy the old wolf prowling

the women peel themselves, and preen
this midsummer looms long, warm, pristine
shorts the norm, halter tops, and toe-nails
the lessons to be learned, what life entails

a dim lit bar, dark wood, the jukebox shuffled
that's the life i choose, my tee shirt ruffled
jeans old and faded, shirt cotton, and worn
my feet sandal shod, my hair yet unshorn

i sit and wait here for the talk to begin
my friend is coming, my friend, not my kin
i sit, replete in place, my mind abuzz

i wait for beginning, new thought to be
others to reflect, to listen, to validate me
and that is what i do, just cuzz

murphy watching passy approach

there is a space for each of our own needs
uniquely proportioned and with room
enough for us to fill, or clean with broom
flying, stirring the motes like sowing seeds

there has to be floor enough to locate
to land separately and then to grow
in one's own way, there has to be a wind to blow
up around, to whirl, it is difficult to relate

the lack of human closeness thus implied
people crowd around, that's what makes people
and undoes them too sometimes in the night

the city, that's where it's hardest, we've dyed
our ceilings a cloudless blue, the steeple
we worship under is vaultless and tight

murphy seeking direction as a sufi dervish

the oil of midnight lamp dimly thinks
lights unfinished walls within my home
shadows shape a fantasy to come
a certainty that in me slowly sinks

my shirt unbuttoned bares a beating heart
keeping time where no one else can see
no caring eye to know the quick of me
discern the bloody sea lanes of my chart

no sleep yet beckons mind that's held atop
the slumping form that sits in its repose
whose spark still tongues the ache of losses past

no answer found til thought can stop
and hands can reach to touch, and close
around another's warmth again at last

murphy in a three bedroom apartment, alone

river calm, a slow slipping majesty
summer's canopy, a speckled dark green
time settles to stillness in air's pregnant hum
looking to far shore for what i have seen

last night's rain has kept freshness in ground
water's waves glitter a quick glimpse of sea
mind settles byways atop slip of slide ways
i smell deep of my sweat, smell deep of me

raucous boats spread their arrows upstream
quarreling friends wag tongues in brusque banter
small snippy dogs sniff around my calm space

i wonder to self, am i dreaming a dream
sure of my waking safe back in home bed
sure of my being, sure of my place

murphy watching the river of always

my coat finally adequate to winter's cold
i bravely stand with you, unbuttoned, loose
enough to kiss and hold your hand in line
waiting for an elephant to take you home

the other waiters make some room for us
they tacit share our joy and innocence
melted snow seems missing on such a night
and sky seems warmer in its broadway light

we talked to remember the just before
that happened as we wanted, and as bright
as the coming glare of the bus headlight

that plunges to meet searching eyes in sight
and swoops down to make our last words bold
with touching, and turning, on stage, just right

murphy the museum raconteur

there was a time when my blood ran hot
my limbs were lithe in their early spring
that was the time when i took my shot
to bring life's bell to a thrilling ring

i know this now as my thoughts grow old
that what that was was my chemistry
the well run road that my father's told
by their mastery of the mystery

i accept what is and hoe the ground
i live upon, it's where i belong
i walk the road that's been walked before

i look behind then i look around
i think a while then i sing my song
then when i look i can see the more

there was a tot of wine, now gone
which swished upon effulgent lips
now burgeoning red, alone
without their mates, their salty sips

i note the sky was clear, though dense
with cooling haze of winter chill
and far from here, the inside here
the place in where i make most sense

you left to me, the outside me
a glow effusive in its joy
in curling, lonely slide to sleep

you left also, an inward tow
of thought which dreams will shape
to loving, touching deep, down deep

murphy starting a new journal late at night

and when the moment comes, it's there
accept its complex gift
and when another comes, it's there
pay attention to it now

ground the thought in memory
root firm its thereness
smell the color of its moment
embed the sweatiness of life

fix the words in concrete
then toss them overboard
to fall beneath the waters
and drown beyond the noise

and when the moment comes, it's there
pay attention to it now

murphy with non-euclidean parallels

this winter lurches on with a special timidity
a thaw that seems eternal in its effect
no snow, nor sleet here, on this coast, this year
just rain that comes with strength, then goes

i hardly button my coat these days, no hat
no glove, nor scarf, just me, two thickish shirts
both open to flash my inner t-shirt glee
the skin below soft cotton nearly free

i wonder as i walk, and bask in southern sun
how life has brought my past to live with me
hot texas sun of all my youthful sweat, here now

i shudder when i think, all cozy in my evening robes
how death shall bring its time to be with me
no matter sun, nor cold, nor all the other worlds that be

murphy working on his strum for cajun stomps

time idles as i open my appliance
i still call it icebox and turn off its juice
i chop a while as if to peak beneath
let loose the source beneath the frozen stream

all the crusted cold of loss
all the aches in stiff old bones
to squat again, pick rocks and grin
a foolish boy in his foolish joy

but now i wait for the ice to break
for spring to return to my warm shod feet
for time to seep a warmth into my cave

i stoop to sop cold swamp of floor
the flow of life slips slow in thaw
within my cave and behind my door

murphy whiling away his afternoon

when hours move into the fall of one's soul
to stain and scar in stabbing haunt of night
the heart alone holds considered hours of old
in worlds retained while passing through the light

and moments pass but still remain inside
the everlasting home of memory
and moments stare and prove they haven't died
as glances last for all eternity

hours reflect as scenes come slow to view
become objects, blur, are yet realized
thoughts become joy, time is savored, renewed
and all forgetting now is now revised

this ink reflects those stabs, those scars, those stains
those moments hung on walls within my pains

murphy taking his first baby steps

when i was very young i walked the path of autumn
now that i am old i seek the rains of spring
the very heights i reach serve new as bottom
contain my shyness in the forwardness i bring

the river of my dreams wells its way up hill
the ship i sail upon dives into the deep
the troughs between the waves too broad for me to fill
and when i'm most aroused i lay me down to sleep

it's always been that way the sense i have of life
no matter what i want the opposite arrives
comes sidling in the scene without a welcome cue

i have almost given up, i almost tell my wife
it's just too much to take, the dullness of my knives
the edges of unsharpened blades cutting new

murphy left-footed and right-handed

when the evening meal approaches and mind
can turn to softer needs, i so indulge
my moods that winding down means winding up
the fantasies that make this life worthwhile

i sometimes wander straight with faculties
full sailed, intact, with clear intent and eye
but more often i will damp direction's fire
and meander in an imagined cove

the haze descends, and soundings take my soul
past manufactured shoals of sublimity
whether gas or liquid, solid smoke, or

whatever seems to broaden, thus limit
me, it's tasted as peculiarity
those hidden reefs now fixed to my marrow

murphy ritually dying as a shaman must

when younger i wished to talk to betters
in years, and i thought, in their perceptions
the words never came; and tongue-tied i tried
to force my message by overt strutting

a physical presence and not facile
curlicues of learned expressiveness
unformed letters had an urgency felt
by this sender as need to be well read

i now know the futility of this
normal reaction to a child's frustration
the abnegation of that thing strived for

i am now teacher of exactly what
i was before, in years, in perceptions
and blocked still by apprehension of words

murphy outlining his thesis project

winter will not wait its proper time
glare coats wires with the ice of intelligence
breaks them with its cold weight
it coats bare limbs, smashes power lines

world dank and bleak this mid-december
streaky clouds, orange from the rising sun
crisp late year air pulled deep into lungs
bundled workers scurry along their daily way

my amble slow, attentive; eyes, nose, ears aware
dreams still within from the night, and from long before
imbuing place with palpable depth, with purpose

thoughts piling their mist into pomp and grandeur
stacking layers of goals sore waiting achievement
all possible now in the throes of wintry intent

murphy determined and defiant until the end

yellow stab of jonquil peeks through snow
still lingering despite the thaw of spring
color needed for the thought of change to come
the health of warmth that summers bring

a lemon skin crushed touches mind as tart
fresh thought of heat and flesh exposed to sun
the yellow beckons in the stacks of fruit
flown into a northeast winter on the run

i taste this yellow sense when i see it fresh
when eyes can touch what hands will reach to hold
i sit and work with rhythms i now know cold
and press within to warmth of heart and flesh

i trust myself, and you alone, and us together
to share the magic next three months of weather

murphy shivering a syncopated song of love

all i have left is an occasional thought
bubbling from below, burgeoning in the mind
acting as reality of an appropriate kind
a confirmed suspicion, an actuality caught

a determined expression making itself known
pushing past parity to a soft eruption
a smell that penetrates far beyond form
an accumulated distinctness all its own

i talk to it now, i listen to it speak
the synapses acrickle with their code
sending forth fingers to their task

i am old, decrepit, though still far from weak
as i ease into song which is always the mode
the intricacy of ink flow a sureness of mask

murphy about to venture to china

dancing on heads

seven imps improved their slippery grasp
on reality dancing in the ink of my pen
first they agreed to improve their stature
in debating how they could all stand there

gawking at the liquid pouring of their selves
appreciating the twinkle in their spirit
matching impressions of their impossible
willfulness manifest in my cramped scrawl

and they did persist, and by imposing
a strict order of listening, their glee
glinted as they took turns of attention

improbably enough no angels came
to dispute primacy of importuning
implosions inherent in my imp's souls

murphy persisting in his odd habits

a confusing fall warbler chanced outside
this dusky room yesterday, as i sat
to sort my flitting thoughts in papered shapes
to flip when i wish to see reflection

this rather small green and yellow bird
hopped into my senses as his perception
of changes on the way south prompted
movement and lack of delineation

my movement has been the opposite
direction, and more slow, but the blurring
of outline has come about even as
cold achievement has been forced to keep warm

my life so far shows how the harvest time
is tinged with a faded singular me.

murphy always the solipsist

a poem ceases to be as soon as it is
written, my random thoughts become this page
and perchance read, reacted to
by those who have a similar sickness
the need to confront a bourgeoning sense
of compatibility of image
their feelings at that time of word sounding
wrest final concreteness from my intent

but that is far off and unheard as i sit
selecting from my smoky wraiths of form
hearing in my graphite pencil a bell
calling to attention the worship i feel
toward squiggly lines and amorphous thought
a pealing to my special sense of now

murphy talking to himself again

long lazy western sunny afternoons
set atop the latest hightowered forms
we let glass keep march coolness at arm's
length, we allow nascent warmth into our room

we soak in closeness of atmosphere
wine gets duskier as dimming light
slants closer to horizon, to farthest sight
my patience of place is especially here

this round table, these knobbly sane people
make a oneness, a fit, which transcends
awkward angles which they exude

ask yourself, is the morrow less stippled
with fineness, less complete in what might be
than the truth learned today without chatter

murphy young, brash, and given to chatter

LSD-25

memory and sight are equalities
the world experienced free as now with then
an earthly fire from simple vastness fed
flaring in view the same as ashes blown
the mind's pseudopods splitting for each birth
branches reaching everywhere without roots
leaves curlless to sun's all-pervading girth
growth with time the will for love's rebirth

no aching smartness felt as one's own
peculiarly individual path
no magnetic compass with which to hone
each lost directional which i ran
the intelligent being of itself
an infinite series converging

my passion has not time to spend, trying
itself with hours not often here to feel
the offered presence of your source appeal
needs documentation, if not dying

in the elizabethan sense of fair hand
to be the sense of being fair to me
to come to be the all welcoming sea
and thus, of course, to bring my heat to land

ah yes, there seems a seam to such a sew
as awkward tailings shrink to withered naught
and when finished with the fulsome sow of such

there might be still the soured mash of woe
betide the one who unaware be caught
drinking beer and idly making much of much

murphy indulging in a mixing of drunken metaphors

small sapsuckers peer through dusty slant of sun
call back when i match my sounds with their woods
the mood settles with motes of spring pollen
the afternoon becomes the total trees

i hear the rustle of young growth bestir
feel the river rumble in the distance
eye deer asleep in their dappled shadows
taste air rich with global energy

i trace paths of small mammals in my mind
set snares at appropriate places
think along the ridges as hawks meet dusk

haul my physicality back to fire
and food to share with those i've shared before
my return takes ages to task my love

murphy letting loose his shyness

sometimes cambridge overdevelops her stalks
holding, twisting, nurturing them far too long
a sick city of wavy brick sidewalks
slashing young students with her siren's songs

but masking all her scars, why look at me.
my countenance seems smooth, but my gait's not
oh, it`s not for drink i walk crooked, see
inside my brain, gnarled-up old hickory knot

don't you wish you were half as sick as i
stealing back to harvard year after year
doesn't it make you sad enough to cry
that you can never feel, never have my fear

that someday cambridge after all her kissing
will bend very low and whisper, be missing

murphy wondering what the wide world holds

sometimes in january, sometimes later
false spring addles winter's slow movement
an unexpected warmth greets the waiter
for change, for inevitable improvement

too soon the sun, too near the beginning
of the year, before soil's scheduled rest
has been completed, for the full meaning
of fallow to have been put to the test

some things should come in their own good time
unforced, unhurried, unfolding their grace
with measured tread to ineluctable rhyme
a stately reasoned tempo to proper place

take care that first glimpse of summer sun
doesn't lure the leap before groundwork's done

murphy plowing the back forty again

the crowds have lain basted, spitted anew
for full summer's heat to brown them to languor
each early june's warmth has stripped them for view
now fall's sweet crispness has brought its cold danger

there's no parachute jump nor merry-go-round
nor boardwalk stuffed now with those shaded eyes
no deliberate attempt to record the sound
of nubility's slow slick smooth demise

just the sea's soft acceptance of land's salt
as runoff rain's downhill careen adds slow
to years of life dissolved by no man's fault
just minutely measured increase caused by flow

of tears themselves, no real salty smartness
below the eye-trails of crusted apartness

murphy letting the waves do their soothing

the light is blinding outside my dank study
on the windowed side of my thoughts of course
as i sit in physical idleness, scuddy
doubts are shadows on my plains of gorse

for i grow such spiny plants in my mind
steadfastly turned toward the panelled rear
of my chosen place-- to sort my own kind
from the obviousness of all those others near

for they can never know nor feel my damp
apprehensive palmy sense of loneness
the small "i" of knowing my apartness
so i turn from experience, sights, lamps

carried by my friends in their forlornness
to find my own heartfelt human shortness

murphy chem lab specialist in old streubenmueller high

i come into my room, i come alone
the guests have left me here and so has she
as now she must, and now as i, to be
must be beside my self, be next to bone

i have no other ness, no other thing
to bring to here, when i retire at last
when i no longer have the prop of past
in practiced doing what time itself might bring

i have only that one small thing, my self
the this of what i am and thus might be
the then of what i alone might bring to bear

i come tonight and know the book and shelf
wherein there lies within this lock the key
alone i sit, and talk to you, i share.

murphy at home in his odd shaped room

i stand fast in this cold, this night
the recent warmth of wine returns to me
i'm fleshed and more through fresh propinquity
you've turned around and now you're gone from sight

my kith and kin are falling, as will i
and you who taught me fresh to want anew
will stoop to know the bitter root i chew
when your time comes to bring the others' sigh

i stand alone and watch the ones who watch
and talk to us of how we sparkling show
our youth as feelings written smiling loud

white billows, love is frosty breathy cloud
joy's warmth holds tight, tight yet leaking slow
i turn and see my days, another notch

murphy newly aware of how precious taste can be

the sun peeks out from its place of growing
it stabs the heart of this river's flow
it seeks my heart upon my waking
the light reveals what i should know

the water's wash takes all my feeling
the waters' soak my aches away
the light of current sprinkles fresh thought
i look again through glinting show

how like a child to seek for mother
much like the christian search for soul
is never more than this fresh light

i know the fresh cold wind of moving
then i am out and my being slows
and i look outward to end of night

murphy full of birth feelings

cock crows in my adopted father's yard
arthritic hunting dog sleeps at my feet
dreaming of scents denied and hunts undone
the city encroaches on how we've lived

or ought to have lived in our special ways
the back porch is streaked with the chicken's shit
stained with patches of new laid concrete
the trees look sickly in their pruned setting

i remember, seem to never forget
the readings of youth, the days spent inside
experiencing other's impassioned rites

my coming of age resembled facile color
engendered in forced hothouse bloom
pure in its not unexpected joy.

murphy watching his favorite, the banty rooster

i was lying yesterday afternoon,
quietly, drinking beer, staring through the
window which was streaky as often we
ourselves seem to become, lying, immune

through crazed glass i spied a contrailed plane
easing its way from top of my view to
bottom, at first i focused as the blue
surroundings wavered, the air was insane

the jet split in two, dipped and dived left
then right, but never together, and eyes
followed lazily this arbitrary sun

perhaps the beer, perhaps the times themselves
made duality seem the lesser lie
made contentment complete, metaphor fun

the order of brilliance is the web fresh caught
in pearly sheen quivering in the wind
the spider's trap spanning thick path
constricted wholeness sucking water from the air

the scheme this knitting thread of worlds
the special reddening from the east
that flashes in mind when thoughts fall and clot
and inky finger speaks feast of time full caught

a shudder shakes the touching eye of morning
begins at head, sinks to arms, slides down
the person helpless in its path to ground

a rhythm wraps the writhing meat for death
the spider ends his moment's light
web swept clear of tears without a sound

murphy drifting helpless on the waves

5 exploded Sonnets

elaine choy's ode

each time we begin anew as a dream
loving before we have the consciousness
asking ourselves too soon about the hurt
in part acting out of those fantasies

needs reflected in their overt telling
echoes unwanted as we listen hard
chanting that which we most have told thus heard
heeding not the past we have both subsumed

our startled awareness brings back freshness
yesterday tastes tart as though new grown now
some semblance of order cannot be borne

our cultured astuteness standing tall proud
defending the depths we shall soon attain
eliding fulsome recompense we share

each time we begin anew as a dream
our tentative movements awkward, unformed
ten to carry us forward to some
misunderstood bliss, hoped for perfection

there is acknowledgement of that full past
accentuating aspects of feeling now
acceptance of the relevance of time
an easement of the soul in ever changing sea

the attraction is indisputable
forcing us to face prematurely that
possessive drive for the ultimate one

we should be wary of the birth of hope
which leads too simply to a form of life
loving before we have the consciousness

loving before we have the consciousness
of that love, before we've even begun
the complex modulations required for
expressing what intuition still gives
leads again to possibilities fraught
with uncertainty. we leap forward fresh
not knowing where the soft land lies, richly
nurturing growth despite seeds' random fall
the fear of cold, a weather change, denies
proper joy in the purblind rightness
in bravely reaching for the returning sun

the realities of seasons intrude
as we use learned logical life models
asking ourselves too soon about the hurt

asking ourselves too soon about the hurt
we assume must come whenever people
conjoin in as couples to explore selves
together and alone, will assuredly
bring that hurt as inevitable, lock
patterns of future dance to already
learned foibles, prevent the very health
needed if we will somehow muddle through
successfully achieving a settled
existence which supports and nurtures

our awarenesses permit a flowering
which can only be appreciated
in freedom from fear, in presence of hope,
in part acting out of those fantasies.

in part acting out of those fantasies
we so deeply crave we cannot show them whole
our usual diffidence departs, weaving
jagged edge where seamlessness should be

where the process promoting acceptance
of open search begins to feel as if
it fits into where our march has always
been headed had we but paid attention

had we but taken the time to slowly
set the scenes bit by bit, the landscape
whole so felt in the shaping that wills
would became ways of relating in homey
comfort the full depth of those untoward
needs reflected in their overt telling

needs reflected in their overt telling
we strut and prance with practical abandon
highlighting what we think we wish to be done
those edges don't cut through to the quick
sense of impending change, they rather mask
true modes of excitement, true indices
of feeling with conventionability
the already learned responses for show.

gain comes when real problems are discussed
heard by all parties, perhaps misunderstood
but dealt with with faith in up front dealing

listening to the other response than
that which was expected or even wished
echoes unwanted as we listen hard

echoes unwanted as we listen hard
replace expected harmonies and clash
with time out of sorts, the biorhythm
unsensed and counterproductive to thought

the thrust of expression being but first
drafts of ferment, the compassion needed
to halt process in situ to await
reflection, and thus losing purity

the interval permitting rehearing
inhibits smooth flow of ordered discourse
syncopates heart beat to frenetic peals

the attempted fixation of new patterns fails
to deal with old problems, as we are always
chanting that which we most have told thus heard

chanting that which we most have told thus heard
we reproduce our idiocies pell-mell
outlining in gross aspect our worst felt
inadequacies, thus giving them life

it's the background noise which upbraids
our senses, forcing them perforce to heed
formal morality, to be the same
as all we've been told before, ever done

the tricks of memory pin us to all
that's gone before as we have social pressures
presume agreement to all we have told
each other of the ultimate worth
yet it's only surface trick which fixes flux
heeding not the past we have all subsumed

heeding not the past we have all subsumed
we march proudly forward to similar
fates-- compromise with composure with luck
downward spiral of suppression if not

we do not pay attention to simple
truths learned repetitively by us all
youth is impatient, old age is hurtful
the middle passage seems to seek the mean

until a happenstance brings it all back
the spilled black paint on patterned hand wrought rug
the crystalline moment of new born sun

muted awareness comes from human wear
which underlines how use forces design
our startled awareness brings back freshness

our startled awareness brings back freshness
we push past usual solicitude
leaving behind our accomplishments when
we with great effort confront our senses

the adumbration of the fervors
raises hackles, if not brings on fevers
raging through the body of the body
left behind in forgotten memories

i talk to several bodies of part
whenever I seek to expand the rule
of thumb opposing sensitive fingers

as boldness will establish true touch
my rude steadfastness brings me back once more
yesterday tastes tart as though new grown now

yesterday tastes tart as though new grown now
the tangle of youth tautens in visits
an effort at recapture can caption
wildest scene with an understood tang

a cyclical view of mankind is old
and subtle in its permissive bias
allowing for hope born in the despair
attendant on all attempts at progress

i went again to work today to find
solace of sorts in good deeds, those selfish
manifestations of cruel morals

the crush which awaits the child we once were
falls full force in storm of encirclement.
some semblance of order cannot be borne

some semblance of order cannot be borne
within the mind when time should disappear
when cause ceases affecting actions
when events take solidity from themselves

not from linkage have we learned to presume
nor from artificial codes of behavior
do we progress in our confrontation
with divinity to oneness we share

beneath it all, below our discerning
hearts, behind our masks, between lines on show
begins the awareness of rectitude

the forwardness of the manners we live
the changing role age assumes in aging
our cultured astuteness standing tall, proud

our cultured astuteness standing tall, proud
finally allows the outline its grace
Its redundant themes to intermesh
in spiraled pointedness, in recurrent modes

ultimately to a piercing sameness
a brotherhood of shared humanity
we allude to this more often as we
look again and yet again at pattern

nature has decreed our movement from salt
seas to sugared thoughtful ease, from struggled
survival to intense concern with how

we struggle to maintain the quality of our selves
the ones we juxtapose to probe our feelings
defending the depths we shall soon attain

defending the depths we shall soon attain
we often neglect the growth required
to sustain the attempt, to decide on
plumbing to deepest fathom; and we forget

how seldom does choice allow pleasure
its fullness; how sad that delimiting
existence permits survival while stab
at totality beguiles sanity

instinctively we grasp this double bind
life entails, we look deliberately
away from consequence inherent

in the absurd, we help ourselves delude
each other in manner of love's telling
eliding fulsome recompense we share

eliding fulsome recompense we share
we plow onward to reach our beginning
the completely nurtured warmth of sharing
life's bloody basics, the throes of each birth

the inescapable pain of each death
the lone struggle for individual
understanding of recurrent process
as payment for intense moments of bliss

we step back at times in a ritual
attempt at evocation of cycles
we focus our entangling logical
development; we add density in
colors of irrational feeling drives
each time we begin anew as a dream

spring

to come fresh each spring is to be the child
open to the world to close inner form
patterning ourselves on growth's primal charm
asking how intricately nature has styled

madness returns as color brings morning sun
exciting the dormant feelings to life
luring vibrance with light's broad stabbing knife
arriving from low angle in shadowed run

corners of darkness gradually yield
health of unique, glowing, exampled views
appearances controlled as well as new grown

narrow byways thus slowly revealed
in exposing dark shunts to further bemuse
numinous reflection being the seeds we've sown

spring I

to come fresh each spring is to be the child
kneeling in the mud new thawed and formed
from a hard fastness to a flesh wetness
to the sucking, slaking force of turmoil's surface

to be both sire and practitioner, to be
unseen underneath milking raw face
of ideas--- to be roots sustaining growth
to be change required to be seductive be

to be form, seed, the guile of reception
to embody chance in proper surroundings
to be chosen as happenstance enriched

to bring magic and beauty of season
in an inevitable forced explosion
open to the world to close inner form.

spring II

open to the world to close inner form
we bespeak consolidation of purpose
the effortless reconstruction of the new
particularities enjoined by now to other time

yesterdays, tomorrows, strings of nows
are our whens, ultimately sorted out
reflected upon within the framework
our own choosing within fresh uncertainty

we pinpoint a moment as meaningful
absorb its inner force before the collapse
leads to the next indelible balance

we chance by focused light on etching sea
swimming lonely midst tempting enchantments
patterning ourselves on growth's primal charm

spring III

patterning ourselves on growth's primal charm
we ask acceptance of contradiction
and the saying of what we do, do not wish
to happen in symmetry of the telling

what will finally flourish does not begin full vigored,
nor can the spindly child be pruned
to immediate knowledge of its bloom
no, the thrall of self is trying

i ask again what is the goal, what end
does man presume, which of the many thoughts
he's held lead to the higher ground of love

i ask if the much used words have life
whether assumed plumage is mime, or mask
asking how intricately nature has styled

spring IV

asking how intricately nature has styled
beguiles the shaping hand in soil's dream
turns the earth to loosen its packed sense
elicits a fond use of its presence

and once this groundwork's well laid and over
once the chosen shoots have been well started
comes the battle to prevail, to become
in worldly struggle an answer found new

it is always so with what is wanted
it looms large in sleepless night of desire
and takes form in blind hand's grasping sight

it's feeling flesh become flesh at first light
in groping closure on fresh immediacy
madness returns as color brings morning sun

spring V

madness returns as color brings morning sun
soft grey remembrance is hanging plant wall
the scene through wickered pane grows natural then
reflects first sights from before we were born

a faith in complex nuanced feeling grows
details creep, fill the dark masses slowly
slowly, a relentless sense of total show
begins awareness of flooded whole time

there is surcease which steals upon the lonely
small early hours of our person, we touch
love that begins the long learning process

paused in our slumber, we slowly rouse hand
to soured heat of close entangled soft form
exciting the dormant feelings to life

spring VI

exciting the dormant feelings to life
we probe our inconsistencies, sense
in those differing faces ways to be
which lead to memories buried hard-by

and our eyes glimpse at odd moment,
when time seems a rocky creek in its onward flow
a stretching of froth as bubbly cover
an iridescent, pristine happening

the cold runoff from mountainous fastness
seems most alive then, burbling in careen
splashed as awakening handily tossed

as dawning, as purification rite
as harbinger of sun's full liquid growth
luring vibrance with light's broad stabbing knife

spring VII

luring vibrance with light's broad stabbing knife
we rouse ourselves early to catch the sheen
the future, a dimness imperceptible
outlined, a felt looming presence made manifest

at last a beginning with heart at hand
a singing first reach of echoic soul
there can be no other response to self
as loss of onset peals reluctant toll

those memories of night become as real
as recall, made alive most when we accept
the view of dreams we've all held far down

we are lulled to quiescence within the eye
belying repetitive dark acceptance of storm
arriving from low angle in shadowed run

spring VIII

arriving from low angle in shadowed run
possibilities abscond as our fears do
scampering before the illumination
the primeval moment taking to itself

an awakening arrives, blurs edge's beginning
becomes consciousness, the far horizon
a greyness suddenly transformed into shards
the color of our quickness full blooded

and, sighted, we slow appreciation, so seeing
can be unblinking calm, so it becomes
our seeking feelings in their nurturing fullness

as this new found skin is spread to surround
unblocking directness with its massive tent
corners of darkness gradually yield

spring IX

corners of darkness gradually yield
to this time's inexorable advance
in the sweep of experiential data
overwhelming in immediacy of its flying

but behind fusty drapes of our further needs
reason lies, as we have so often assumed
it stacks splintered words next to proper response
as we leave in the rush to fully begin

passage is crucial if we're to reach home
having understood so finally how safe
our haven must be in mortal guarantee

and this dawning becomes suffusion in birth
of process, and fitness, in its approaching
a health of uniquely glowing exampled views

spring X

a health of uniquely glowing exampled views
which might supersede our every other plan
presupposes a toast for individual efforts
we're programmed to protect self as sanctity

the strength in reaching a decisive state
either in measurement or in leading
lies not in the exercise of ruling
we radiate certainty in our vision

the attention attendant on our honor
asks personally for absurd reason
anger focusses upon an occasion

the furor forces change on balanced cell---
a chance is taken, the telling itself survived
our appearances controlled as well as new grown.

spring XI

our appearances, controlled as well as new grown
burgeon past their purpose without our knowing
and in their passing show pathways chosen
instinctively in purblind feeling drive

we look back to see where we've been going
searching for steerage in this trackless now
we grow as we have been programmed, fathered
and mothered to our estimable ends

we imprint these as ineradicable
arrows, irreversible in their cues---
barbed in their underlined tenacity

disallowing all discursive mistakings
we have this surface as constant direction
narrow byways thus slowly revealed

spring XII

narrow byways thus slowly revealed
we pass them unheedfully, mistiming
our response to some new reality
of our own making, of our own becoming

we can only discover what we are
through homage to this attentive purpose
we seek exploration without the mainstream
we find value as complete reflected calm.

we should value our sight, our eyes, the touch
we bestow; and become bone of those we love
shoring their sensate strengths, carrying our selves

we should beware false openings luring to dead end
we should shed our looming fears
in exposing dark shunts to further bemuse

spring XIII

in exposing dark shunts to further bemuse
the sense we crave of enveloping warmth.
we clasp a tattered covering to hand
a peculiar and vulnerable security

at abruptly learning to survive strangers
who are protecting their own hidden doubts
this secrecy involved in human fear
is experienced, visits past its stay

but recurrent beginning rebirth cycle
brings with acceptance a faith in order
an open trust that offers self to world

the telling then becomes a way to be
constantly mulling an awed sense of now
numinous reflection being the seeds we've sown

spring XIV

numinous reflection being the seeds we've sown
in random miraculous beginnings
a fullness to be is encapsulated
becomes shaped growth to ultimate known end

the replenishment of our animus
treads a thin line bordering on rage
to survive, yet embodying love
encompassing such frustrating pain

the intense pleasure presaging the life
we offer chance, nonchalantly or no
repeats joy basic to our balance

we begin a new process as we change
in restless proving of fertility---
to come fresh each spring is to be the child

summer

the summer brilliance of noon light shimmers
our instincts move from that full directness
past the desire to absorb life's full heat
as we reach growth presumed in kernelled wit

madness itself is invited by all
enrichers of nature's bounty, we tame
love to bear better fruit as we know it
asking not what loose rankness might have brought

charge the sun with fetid air of decay
hail the dreaming green smells carried with us
along with sweating brown skin as we touch

normality flees reason in fullness
impending harvest has rhythmic season
night, never again be so far away

summer I

the summer brilliance of noon light shimmers
in my mind, a palpability is
purpose presents its own reality
fullness of design has become now

there has always been colorful essence
as epitome of fecundity
self perpetuating forms of self
timeliness allows a force of thought

mature fruit of striving escapes
tender beginnings, its obviousness
obscures willed hope necessary to grow

obfuscates others crowded out
in mad thrusting to gather all of sun
our instincts move from that full directness

summer II

our instincts move from that full directness
perceived as antidote to ego's dance
the fearful protectment from impinging
others with their clouding shields of tactics

the assumed guilt of needs we have shared
are our inadvertently ripened fruits
to be taken in full open supping
a conquering of dangered beginnings

the roundness, beauty, and color we attain
seems worthwhile now as a final reflection
of those other achievements, of those passed

and sometimes when the fullness of pattern
shows constricting sameness of heart, we push
past the desire to absorb life's full heat

summer III

past the desire to absorb life's full heat
lies a no-man's land, such fertility
as was never dreamed, to be sown full grown
before its sharing bestows its essence

at the end of endeavor, at the expense
of certitude, we risk our mortal sons
for careful nurturing of new leaves
and tendrils presupposes surprise

to wish to know the fullness of one's worth
while striving is immutably affecting
one's course, begs the question itself of change

A seed is miraculous in its closed
protection, a life's mystery is solved
as we reach growth presumed in kernelled wit

summer IV

as we reach growth presumed in kernelled wit
we begin to marvel at subtle chance
the choice we have made in retrospect
the divergent paths withering channels
carrying the fullness of finality
and making way for realizing the goal
the middle ground of life, the awesome strength
of mature purpose fed by effulgent sun

the rush to reach culmination poised
proudly, shining in total obeisance
eschewing the murky wetness inside
equally necessary to so fatten
direction til it bursts destination
madness itself is invited by all

summer V

madness itself is invited by all
we imagine, thus accomplish, those maps
laid out to chart meandering recourse
exemplify redoubts we hide behind

it's certitude we wish which beguiles
the storied happenstance, highlighting
our worth as singular achievement
inevitable denouement, proudful craze

touching mortal perfection, a portrait
of the moment in purity of style
coming to each man in his trueness to time's

relevance, and what should be a reaching
toward beauty's poised balance, we are
enrichers of nature's bounty, we tame.

summer VI

enrichers of nature's bounty, we tame
the sense we assume becomes manifest
in completion of complex maneuvers
we use the use we put things to to be

our feeling for life, the symbols we share
are manipulated, gathered, pruned, made
to be more than they were before we saw
and unaware decided they could be

we especially form our love's forms
in our minds; we shape what we hope to feel
before us as promised gift, growth and change

to suit our needs we feed other's aspects
that are part of ourselves, we espalier
love to bear better fruit as we know it

summer VII

love to bear better fruit as we know it
persists as never ending surprise
as newly opened flesh of feeling
taking aback willing acceptance, forcing

life is unexpected, even unwanted
rawness rankles, brings attention to bear
on changing shape in retrospective care
after the harvest is full design seen

it's long afternoons of heat, controlled
transformed in slow chemistry of burgeon
as limb bringing life in its completeness

we accept what we find, we transcend selves
at our peril, we face fresh accomplishments
asking not what loose rankness might have brought

summer VIII

asking not what loose rankness might have brought
we place faith in preordained order
within beginnings we unknowing start
finally accept that which we become

we shape the sense we know, what we are
by this acceptance of maturity
we concentrate awareness on its parts
to more fully grasp blotches of the whole

it's never all we wished when end is seen
bringing slow decline from flawed achievement
inexorable sliding off from peak

performance never quite the same
in grace or bold reach, but form always distinctive
charge the sun with fetid air of decay

summer IX

charge the sun with fetid air of decay.
my sturdy trunk begins its sleep, my fruit
stand pure in faded background of nurture,
my broad fanned interest reluctantly leaves

its fulfillment, full fledged trust of season.
slippage is to come, to that complete rest
from inviting growth, change, if it's selfless
somehow achieves that negative balance

sets up tenacity of memory
brings level of feeling sustainable
allows perpetuation of self room

to assume owned point of departure
to grow again in its good time of morn
hail the dreaming green smells carried with us

summer X

hail the dreaming green smells carried with us
in our rummage through life, in our constance
we watch small increments of existence
and pay those attentions necessary

for the continuance of noticed patterns
preordered in the somatic balance
of forebearers, those who carried on long
before our peculiar impingements emerged

in our commingling of felt purposes
we are furthering that which went before
and changing only in our selection

that which we choose to take with us as ours
becomes our heritage, our shared linkage
along with sweating brown skin as we touch

summer XI

along with sweating brown skin as we touch
go our dreams, steaming themselves into pores
in reverse orientation, bypassing
normal function, realistic control

entire being subsumed by protected seeds
surrounded by succulence enticing
consumption; storing is recurrent theme
cutting across obvious grain of time

a realization of memories buried
in vapors beclouding rational outline
the assumption of future becomes now

in good season comes the calm certainty
of fruition, emphasizing how strangely
normality flees reason in fullness

summer XII

normality flees reason in fullness
as rounded form aches for my touching hand
pendulous in its instinct for this time's
destined return, tasted as completeness

the heat lingers past its call for being
burdens reaper with the salt of old wounds
licks liquidly at demonstrated strength
pools its essence in drugged plodding duty

there's too much to do now, days grow shorter
ground provides its fruit unceasingly while
we stagger under imaginative load

there seems no end to this munificence
as the full gushing exhausts its sources
impending harvest has rhythmic season

summer XIII

impending harvest has rhythmic season
we try ourselves in blending well our wills
with nature's there is always the return
of pattern despite singularity
of existence, choice becomes our
weapon for survival, our only hope
of mastery, of tribal enrichment

we now debate certainty of difference
my ways are not yours nor are my daughter's
completely hers, She will be measured more
carefully for having been part of birth

this burden we share from a past choosing
in proud defiance of ultimate cold
night, never again be so far away

summer XIV

night, never again be so far away
let beauty of struggle hone eagerness
to knowing, a constant concentration
sharing each moment's perfection as loss

for we remember not imperfect parts
we select from the maelstrom spinning by
neglecting the lessons af spindly youth
in our haste to prove a singular worth

be with us especially on the heights
of desire, when plucking is mere reaching
to tip of swaying plant patiently there

show ends as beginnings, tell the hard truth
of mirage, reflect on opposites as
the summer brilliance of noon light shimmers

fall

the dropping off is unavoidable
our times run together, each separate
part keeps sounding as all the other's fate,
asking whether our fall is credible

mouldering ground as preferment seems sad
in formal last fitting of nondescript grey
life's peculiarity masking choosing
as eternal leaving what we have had

cold enforced in inevitable sleep
heart sore buried by bruised vegetation
again sense of never again never

night is felt not as abrupt cessation
in ordered schemas for forever
necessary essence is always covered deep

fall I

the dropping off is unavoidable
those left behind are never to become
as ourselves, and we have happened to be
merely preparation for this one time

we seek sureness of quiet steps, answers
leading a trackless way left behind---
choice again, masking necessities
at this moment, when all hurries to some

thought of perfection, where will i choose sleep
rejuvenation through ritual death
a calm preserving of assumed being

for those who might have dissimilar hopes
persist in honoring initiative
our times run together, each separate

faII II

our times run together, each separate
ink its pattern, the river of whole dreams
fulfilled in colorful tangy leavings
the sheer flamboyance of just sleeping life

stoppage first becomes noticeable
as a frenzied zeal of mortality
asking a readiness for last lessons
and an end to fresh possibilities

we check first the others to dare ourselves
all over with an adolescent dread
of being just behind average growth

a few are beginning their stab at the mark
while most are culled before the next round
part keeps sounding as all the others' fate.

fall III

part keeps sounding as all the others, fate
intruding on completely summing up
adding complication in selective
iteration of pattern from new source

we take ourselves as models completely
resolving the forces we impinge on
we neglect frameswork being outfitted
from strange perspective yet meeting our needs

the problem of extension of feelings
cuts two ways and both underline at best
how simple to echo all history

how confining are our optional ways
how quickly we accept cold incursions
asking whether our fall is credible

fall IV

asking whether our fall is credible
begs the issue by praising direction
instead of completeness, cursing waves
instead of curling circumspection of being

truth is both solidly moving and odd
resonance of balanced poise between
extreme manifestations, through thoughtful
probing attempts at prideful resolution

we all fall short of wished for achievement
and escape disasters imaginable
add our magic distance as protection

from ecstacies too painful for any
to maintain, so we accept this, our time
mouldering ground as preferment seems sad

fall V

mouldering ground as preferment seems sad
in the sure appeal of its cool clamminess
we accept too readily denouements
sensed in a tipping to no return

we desire to add essence as enrichment
we become obsessively inevitable
we assume inner workings come unsprung
our terminations become all the same

too soon
        i want one last stand in that sun
named by others for red men, for color
deeply felt and seen as bounteous gift

eschewing the rest waiting patiently
and ritually closing each additional day
in formal last fitting of nondescript grey

fall VI

in formal last fitting of nondescript grey
a distinction shows as leaf's full moment
of descent, a seeming haphazard pattern
of last reckoning, of gene's memory

color as finality, rubicund
fixation of a natural throbbing
unseen, fitful creep to the full green height
of existence in rustling grab for light

those fortunate foes thus left moments free
see strife release its dread precipitate
washing away problematic progress

body cowered today under covered warmth
neglected to renew losing battle
life's peculiarity masking choosing

fall VII

life's peculiarity masking choosing
lies inadvertently along the way
we willy nilly ply our oddnesses
being as there happens a perfect fit

it locks behind, you see, it disappears
with bitter winds sweeping ground's soft gnarled face
just before frost fixes meandering paths
of animal's scurried frenzied searching

there is no preparation, you see, no
anticipating moment of crystal
catching that side which shows only our best

there is only certainty of freezing
our showing gestures, our sharing ourselves
as eternal leaving what we have had

fall VIII

as eternal leaving what we have had
love stands alone: as we hold quicksilver
as we pinpoint ambiguity mldst flush
as fingers point to palms; we miss the point

we stack our wood for winter's long burning
and roughly brush heavy cloaks for our flesh
we focus attention on flame's flicker
drawing out what we so hope to draw in

arms extended to searing warmth we need
does nothing for our nether sides, our other
necessary accoutrements for life's wars

we're left with fading embers and tiredness
a sense of having somehow lost the day
cold enforced in inevitable sleep

fall IX

cold enforced in inevitable sleep
the flakes of purity accumulate
cover our groundwork with inhibiting
perfection; all movement is uniquely shown

as long as fresh patinas aren't added
we grow enured to habitual patterns
it's only the singularity of choice
which is feared, not the trampled known sharing

stubble is given smoothing clarity
awkward angles become unbroken curves
it's only recurrent thaws which still remind

these memories recur past their welcome
fruit has been given, essence will be gone
heart is sore buried by bruised vegetation

fall X

heart sore buried by bruised vegetation
we fester in benumbed isolation
mucking out subterranean nests
while preparing for sparkled slow slippage

it's time for anticipating clear decks
and gravity's swift recall from cold heights
in long blur, our sight a stabbing zag of flurry
in swooping aching achieved as beauty

this first deliberate conquering push
reveals valley's full sweep of pristine hood
hiding life's continued charmed reliance

on layered protection from artful force
of being this constant rhythmic changing
again sense of never again never

fall XI

again sense of never again never
to seek primal form for basic thrust
relying at last on only the past
sketchings for sure intricate magic growth

tap roots in place, or forever denied
ambivalence of purposed probing now
delimited to fertile borders, canvas
primed with chosen subtle hue from known design

now when fear of foreshortening is gone
when perception is proved by honest deeds
comes attentive eye on moment's detail

freeing already felt patterns as once
they were seen, and changed by this fixing time
night is felt not as abrupt cessation

fall XII

night is felt not as abrupt cessation
but as proprietous dark otherness
a needed freeing from the particular
the evidence we've come to begin to see

and the start is as knobbly and stunted
as whorled lopped-off knotty loss of fresh arms
as tender as unbroken linen's limbs
and reaching familiar sameness, never be

disjunct where blind probing will must begin
the small lost momentum starts many lives
to bring an enigmatic immortality

recurrent black patterns reflect as waves
interferent lapping colors distinct
in ordered schemas for forever

fall XIII

in ordered schemas for forever
extend the rolling grids of blind seeing
we search them fitfully with twitching feet
scrabbling after a firmer underpin

for some controlling pivot, to force form
to assume imagining, some ready
row of unused bins to recognize as felt
completeness, for our full fixed discarded wares

the system then become a bordering
of waters' wandering, a shoring up
to delimit flow as regularity

a quiet strength sustaining floating worlds
of fanciful ephemerality
necessary essence is always covered deep

fall XIV

necessary essence is always covered deep
we reach beyond our encrusted vitals
with expendable feelings of person
our hearts as our fears are beribbed and caged

this inaccessability of mind
shading eyes with visored aura of leafy
verisimilitudes, leads to other thoughts
and so beguiles our knowing nothingness

for expanse comes with freshly seen ends
the forgetting of immediate forms
the sensing further sides of childish dreams
the becoming certainty of having been
sharing for now and the requisite time
the dropping off is unavoidable

winter

the sky's malevolence presages shroud
of fast whiteness stretching to cover reach
past times no longer suffice as they teach
a leaden lowering has been allowed

massed consequence looms as ultimate
energy is focussed in dampening
life's force banked by winter happening
as sun's withdrawn symbol of final cut

cold, idiosyncratic, perverse
having formed individual barometer
afflicts all in soft separate ways

needing light again to hold off the worst
i accept center, flickering, final
nurtured by me alone through these hard days

winter I

the sky's malevolence presages shroud
as implacable shield of cold knowing
a sky in nakedness with need unbound
a life as uncontrolled total now

a feverish frenzy belying lost sun
a finality of our summative praise
in inevitable pattern of season's round
return to beginning's fabled endings

the crystalline refrain of happenstance
is frozen as static surface, as clinging
chained liquidity, as rushings stilled

the unique quality of chosen statement
lost in eye's landscaping sense of order
in fast whiteness stretching to cover reach

winter II

of fast whiteness stretching to cover reach
beyond the seeking eye, in such seeing
do we take part when outward mien crinkles
frosts deeper than the springs of life can touch

for the blues and blacks play upon shadows
of old codgers standing with a stillness
for the long glittering bareness so there
an iced shield with colors now grown precious

my senses sigh with the depth of history
seeming in balance now, past sharpness
shown in gentle curve above known serration

past division in parts to measure whole
truth, past privilege as value or prop
past times no longer suffice as they teach

winter III

past times no longer suffice, as they teach
worn images echoing as failures
as background fading into indications
as sketching of underlying details

it's the immediate incongruities
of this now which must be the basic text
allowing our choices life in future
misreadings of known human completeness

patterns then our only saved messages
the sortings of totality as one
memorable act of creation

a full and final inadequacy is
embraced as knowledged vestige of self
a leaden lowering has been allowed

winter IV

a leaden lowering has been allowed
by weight of time's accumulated face
the mists hung in permanent reflection
of many moments wrung from liquid now

they press, these shifting patterns, they press round
each special world's disparate living cells
they press til edges crumble and surface
tension pulls difference back, and sameness holds

they're inside searching for sun's singularity
watching shifting nether side of choice
each one becoming small dispersing shield

each one in itself self-contained aptness
gathering in clusters; while merging inner
massed consequence looms as ultimate

winter V

massed consequence looms as ultimate
form, fixed in circular finality
assuming permanence as shown chrysalis
left in woven place of hidden birth

ends fill beginnings with signal singing
meshing with rhythmic melody saying
yesterdays were tomorrow's nights today
foreseen in resonant ripple's starting

vibrations then, with such short waves, to see
water as image is to blend sound's sight
as surging systolic nurturing now

each being echoing all history's plan
and yet, touching infectious peculiar man
energy is focussed in dampening

winter VI

energy is focussed in dampening
fires of a charcoal fineness, moderation
holding back accelerating rush to ash
a sane controlled use of thinned resources

but burning all the brighter for attention
for giving proper light of scarcity
for holding in hot center of feeling
hoarding for prolongation of duty

bones holding so little aloft, flames flow
whispery now in last tracery
falling in from skeletal powdering

softly with flaked greyness holding outside
they glow slowly in stately ethic care
life's force banked by winter happening

winter VII

life's force, banked by winter happening
leaps forth when least expected, surviving
all attempts at control or harnessing
in manifest self-quirksome being

it lives as husks in patient numbed holding
of otherness than what seems to be near
what obtrudes as slow path of cessation
inward movement freezing to an imagined shell

last lessons are as mute as grasping firsts
and as individual; fumbling structures
felt in the incompletion of their designs

to fill all possible space, persisting
in the already made patterns, fitting
as sun's withdrawn symbol of final cut

winter VIII

as sun's withdrawn symbol of final cut
ice creeps to unprotected warmth, being
dissipates, an overwhelming stillness
protrudes into consciousness, thinking stops

feeling slows til intensity has gone
wind's soul remains, motion, as seeking
as flash of effrontery, as sweeping
as flakes flowing to efface eternity

there is no place discernible as mine
no extension of my sight brings vibrance
no color, no hope of the quick we attend

erasure, rough texture as the only sign
dim remnants of boldest peculiar line
cold, idiosyncratic, perverse

winter IX

cold, idiosyncratic, perverse
it freezes unexpected momentum
and denies life to desireable end
it steals force by stilling true magic dance

i walk a lonely path this day of time
placing careful foot on earth's frosted way
those left behind, those gone away, it's they
who cheer my huddled form its gentle sway

this summing up, this stab at totality
for my last great sore need suffices
to free the sense in quick melting memory

as shared monument, as living out one's will
we peer from pellucid ground with heavy mien
having formed individual barometer

winter X

having formed individual barometer
we charge senses with a practical abandon
and lose nothing which might be savored, saved
while been is in its formative stage

we vary interest now as minutiae glint
unexpectedly call for their true resolvement
as a timely wrapping of feeling chance
in package having need of no other time

we thus allow play scales of certitude
which weigh heavy as accumulated flint
slowly sparking advance of final fear

and our last desparate choices scatter
contained full-stopped memories resounding
afflicting all in soft separate ways

winter XI

afflicting all in soft separate ways
thoughts grow short in felt will of their purpose
and see inescapable newness of death
in fresh cessation of self each has known

within careful frame of total enfolding
an acceptance of otherness: so do i know
a total enjoining so void as is black
and full as is feeling for all that belongs

we hasten to flower each sense of our being
when being is taken so finally away
we stop in our frenzy of ordered preparing

we choose as reaction an acting to steady
the whispery whisking to clear path of days
needing light again to hold off the worst

winter XII

needing light again to hold off the worst
i await slate dawn in this dark freezing
winds of change ever reaching to the time
awaited now with watchful eye expectant

the blue blurred gray of being just now seeing
finely etches sense of one more day
one more leading round of beauty's rising
all important breath of life to stay

now is dread of cold's sure sore succeeding
reaching for a last true stoppage--- moving
so like the ways of love self cauterized

there is no other now can share my feeling
alone with these my hardly trickling lives
i accept center, flickering, final

winter XIII

i accept center, flickering, final
breath of resonant being softly there
in hoarded safety of stately ash
fluffed to baffle tearing, gathering wind

hunkered in practiced ease, shifting slightly
sensing unseen vagary come as sealing
of each few views which remain outstanding
before decrepit vision of my mind

at last no worry for other mourning
no sense of morrow's self-creating love
held to steady hold, thinking on this time

there is crumbling sharpness now to vision
making real these precious feeling's givings
nurtured by me alone through these hard days

winter XIV

nurtured by me alone through these hard days
eternal sense of self is reassertive
waking pain of feeling's formful being
just the growing awe of cutting edge

chopping through thick thread of all my knowing
stopping all additions for this pattern
playing to curtained time in all its flowing
falling before my eyes have lost their glow

i check around and manage meaning's message
and look to see what dawn will soon portend
the light before the light will surely show

as much as ever was to be uncovered
is here today and ever has been here
the sky's malevolence presages shroud

Made in the USA
Middletown, DE
26 February 2023

25490217R00166